Living Landscapes

Parkland

First published in Great Britain in 2002
The National Trust Enterprises Ltd
36 Queen Anne's Gate
London
SW1H 9AS
www.nationaltrust.org.uk/bookshop

ISBN 0-7078-0323-3

Cataloguing in Publication Data is available from the British Library

Art Directed by Wildlife Art Ltd/www.wildlife-art.co.uk
Designed by Reg Page

All colour artwork by Dan Cole/Wildlife Art Ltd

Cover designed by Yellow Box with original artwork by Alison Lang

Printed and bound in Italy by G. Canale & C.s.p.A

Living Landscapes

Parkland

Graham Harvey

THE NATIONAL TRUST

Contents

Autumn colours in the ancient park at Knole, Kent

ACKNOWLEDGEMENTS

Many people have contributed to this book. I am greatly indebted to helpful and knowledgeable staff at National Trust properties throughout the country. Special thanks go to Adrian Clarke, Vikki Forbes and the National Trust team at Hatfield Forest for providing me with a glimpse of this inspirational landscape at a time when much English parkland remained closed as a result of foot-and-mouth disease. I am also grateful to the National Trust conservation team at Cirencester for their generous help and support, and to Jill Butler and her colleagues at the Woodland Trust for their helpful comments. Thanks are also due to James Parry of the National Trust's publishing department, whose encouragement, advice and wise editing has made this a better book than it otherwise would have been. Finally, I must thank my wife Anne for travelling with me on so many journeys of discovery into the British countryside.

A spotted flycatcher darts
after a passing insect.

FOREWORD

One of the greatest joys of the British countryside is the sheer variety of different landscapes it contains. From upland moors to estuaries and ancient woodland to water meadows, this diverse web of scenery and habitat ranks among our most valued treasures. Landscapes inspire on so many levels – whether investigating an aspect of local history or simply walking for the pleasure of it, the same landscape can provide satisfaction in many different ways.

Our personal experience of landscape usually depends on where we live, but there can be few of us who do not feel some sort of connection with parkland. Whether this stems from childhood afternoons spent feeding the ducks in the local town park, enjoying the parkland of our ancient forests or from country house visits, parkland is deeply engrained in our personal and collective experience. The National Trust is privileged to care for many parks, each with their own history and personality. I hope that Graham Harvey's excellent account of the story of parkland will both inform and inspire us all to explore them further.

Fiona Reynolds
Director General, The National Trust

Chapter One

❖

An enduring landscape

AN ENDURING LANDSCAPE

In the shadow of London's Stansted Airport lies Hatfield Forest, a stretch of countryside which in many senses looks little different from the days when King Henry I and his nobles hunted the royal deer there in the twelfth century. It contains wooded areas, many of them surrounded by ancient earth banks, together with patches of scrub – a tangle of bramble, hawthorn and long grass through which young trees are starting to emerge – and areas of open grassland dotted with large old trees. Oak, ash, hornbeam, field maple, beech, crab apple and the scarce English elm are all represented here, and one can also find impressive specimen hawthorns. Most of the trees are pollards, and some of the older trees in Hatfield Forest have been managed in this way for generations. Their massive trunks or boles have grown gnarled and misshapen, many of them becoming hollow as the heartwood decays.

To walk among these ageing giants is to walk in a countryside that feels strangely familiar. This is not the dark, dense forest of fairy tales. It is a bright, open landscape in which individual trees stand out in all their eccentric glory. In his diary for 1876 the Reverend Francis Kilvert described trees like these in a landscape equally ancient – Moccas Park in Herefordshire. To him the great, old trees were 'those grey, gnarled, low-browed, knock-kneed, bowed, bent, huge,

Hatfield Forest is an outstanding example of remnant ancient woodland and wood-pasture; thirty-six species of native tree and shrub are found here, as well as many types of rare plant.

(Previous spread) A classic parkland scene at Ilam in the Peak District. The tranquillity of the landscape belies the often turbulent history of Britain's parks.

strange, long-armed, deformed, hunchbacked, misshapen oak men that stand waiting and watching century after century, biding God's time'.

Kilvert's landscape of ancient trees is one that appears familiar even today. It is the landscape we know as parkland, with its broad stretches of open grassland and large, mature trees. It provides a sense of space and freedom, yet at the same time it can be comfortingly intimate. Ecologists call this kind of countryside wood-pasture, and in many parts of the world it has provided people with a home and a living for a very long time indeed. The term wood-pasture – also known as pasture-woodland – is used to describe a variety of landscapes in which trees co-exist with large grazing animals, whether these be domestic livestock or deer (or both). In most circumstances the establishment of new trees and the presence of large herbivores is incompatible, in the sense that as soon as the shoots of young trees emerge they are browsed off. As a result, new trees rarely become established, the area effectively being maintained as open grassland.

However, in areas of wood-pasture selected trees are managed in ways that prevent animals from doing them serious damage. In most cases they require protection during the initial seedling and sapling stages but, once mature, will thrive in their pasture setting, with the grazing animals preventing the establishment of further new trees (which would otherwise turn the area into

woodland). The number of grazing animals in a set area of wood-pasture is usually higher than would occur naturally in woodland, and it is the influence of large animals grazing or browsing on the lower foliage which determines the appearance of this landscape. It may be very open, with large gaps between the trees and virtually no 'understorey' of shrubs, or – where the density of grazing animals is lower – there may be clumps of trees, with occasional thickets of bramble or gorse in which seedling trees can survive long enough to become established.

Through the ages the owners of wood-pasture have been able to take an annual harvest from both the animals and trees sustained by this landscape, and whilst wood-pasture is known in many parts of the world, nowhere has its management reached the degree of sophistication found in lowland Britain. It is the landscape that has bequeathed to us the concept of parkland, from the urban green space with its swings and play areas to the modern country park, complete with visitor centre and nature trails. It has also given us that pinnacle of British artistic achievement, the landscape park. In one form or another, wood-pasture has been part of the human drama for thousands of years.

Out of the wildwood

Much of the land that is now Britain once lay under continuous tree cover. When the last Ice Age ended in about 11,000 BC the land was recolonised by the vegetation that had retreated south before the advancing glaciers. As temperatures rose at the end of glaciation, the emerging tundra grassland was invaded by successive waves of tree species. First came the cold-tolerant varieties such as birch, aspen, juniper and pine, but as the climate warmed the land was reoccupied by elm, oak and lime, followed by beech, ash, field maple and hornbeam. For thousands of years successive waves of trees made up vast tracts of woodland, barely influenced by human activity and known as the 'wildwood'.

Through much of this period the land was inhabited by groups of wandering hunter-gatherers, who lived off the fruits of the forest. Yet even in this unmanaged environment areas of wood-pasture had begun to appear. Natural events such as fire, storm and drought opened up gaps in the woodland canopy, producing sunlit grassy glades. The tree-felling activities of the beaver also created open spaces, the so-called 'beaver lawns'. Where grazing animals were few in number such grassy areas quickly reverted to scrubland, the nursery for young trees that would restore the closed woodland canopy above. But when large herbivores such as red deer, elk, boar and aurochs – the original wild cattle – gathered in these glades, they would graze off most of the seedling trees almost as soon as they appeared. Through this process the landscape of wood-pasture emerged gradually as a series of islands set in an ocean of woodland. These islands also contained trees of all ages, from young saplings to veterans with hollow trunks and dead branches. Dead-wood was to be found in abundance.

This magnificent ash pollard is one of many outstanding veteran trees in Moccas Park, one of England's finest examples of ancient parkland.

White park cattle are descendants of the aurochs, one of the larger inhabitants of the original wildwood but extinct in Britain since the late Roman era (and globally since 1627).

Early humans would have been very familiar with such places. In these open, grassy areas food animals would have been thick on the ground and life for the hunter-gatherer relatively easy. There was meat to be had in plenty, while the surrounding forest fringes produced wild fruits and nuts, as well as wood for fires. An affinity for the landscape of parkland would therefore have been implanted early in the human mind.

By 3500 BC the wandering tribes had begun to clear woodland using their stone axes, and there is evidence to suggest that these Neolithic peoples were regularly harvesting wood. This would have been done by either, or both, of two different techniques: coppicing and pollarding. Coppicing involves the cutting of the new growth that shoots from the stump or stool of a felled tree. Many native species of tree – including alder, ash, elm, hawthorn, crab apple, hazel and oak – rapidly send up new growth when cut in this way, and the resulting 'poles' can be cropped regularly, usually at between five and ten years of age. Traditionally these poles were used for a variety of functions, ranging from roofing material and fencing to animal fodder. Archaeological examination has revealed that coppiced hazel rods were laid in Neolithic times to form some of Somerset's oldest track-ways, and that many had been cut twice, their tips clearly having been removed in some earlier summer, perhaps to allow the foliage to be fed to livestock. Pollarding involves cutting off the top of the tree at a height of about three metres or at the base of the main limbs. This encourages the regrowth of poles from the open surface. Both coppicing and pollarding became widespread and common methods of harvesting wood, although pollarding was rarely carried out at the regular intervals typical of coppicing – for example, a pollarded oak in Hatfield Forest was only cut seven times, at intervals of between twelve and thirty-six years.

Although the earliest clearers of woodland were probably semi-nomadic herders of livestock rather than settled farmers, the coming of the plough in around 2500 BC led to the gradual destruction of the wildwood. By the time of the Domesday Book (1087), the first known record of the extent of England's forests, much of the continuous woodland canopy had vanished. Furthermore, many of the

Coppicing is a traditional way of harvesting wood. New growth shoots from the stool and the resulting stems or poles are used for a variety of uses ranging from fence posts to roofing struts.

Part of the former Exmoor Forest near Simonsbath in Somerset. Despite their name, many such royal forests contained large tracts of virtually treeless land.

supposedly wooded areas of Norman England were, in fact, regions of wood-pasture. Domesday records show that in the three counties of Nottinghamshire, Derbyshire and Lincolnshire just two per cent of the land area was made up of coppiced woods. However, the proportion of land under wood-pasture was as high as 24 per cent in Derbyshire and ten per cent in Nottinghamshire. Wood-pasture was clearly widespread in Britain at this time, and it formed the principal landscape of the deer parks and chases so enjoyed by the Norman nobles. More importantly, it was the main component of the royal forest, that great gift of the Normans to the English countryside.

The royal forest

Long before the Norman Conquest it had been customary for kings and nobles to hunt wild boar and deer on their own land. Alfred of Wessex was known as 'a mighty hunter', while Athelstan levied as tribute from a defeated Welsh king 'sharp scented dogs fit for hunting wild beasts'. Even the pious Edward the Confessor, who despised most secular interests, 'delighted to follow a pack of swift hounds in the pursuit of game and to cheer them on with his voice'. Yet while they enjoyed 'the chase', the Anglo-Saxons had no specific word for 'forest'. The concept of the 'royal forest' (and the word for it, in the sense that it was wooded land for hunting) was introduced by William I, its purpose being to protect and safeguard the king's venison. The designation of an area of land as royal forest gave the king control over the hunting there, as well as over any tanneries and forges and other resources such as timber and pasture.

At the time of the Conquest every man had the right to hunt wild animals on his own land, subject to a few, ill-defined, game laws. Even when a landowner found others killing his deer or wild boar, he was only entitled to sue them under common law. Offenders suffered only the relatively mild penalty of a fine to the value of the stolen property. William surmised that without tighter restrictions on hunting, game species would eventually be lost, and so within the royal forests he ordered the replacement of common law with the more oppressive forest law. Post-Conquest England was a land of laws, with the new Norman lords having assigned to themselves all the rights and titles of their Saxon predecessors. The feudal system became universal, and with it came the French law that classified people according to their status. The cornerstone of the system was the manor, a term that encompassed both the great dwelling itself and the district around it. At its head was the lord, aristocratic landowner and the king's principal authority and law enforcement officer.

William the Conqueror had a passion for the chase, yet for him hunting was not merely a pastime – it was also a means of keeping his knights-at-arms, in effect his standing army, in a permanent state of war readiness. Hunting was seen as the ideal training for war, and so the creation of royal forests – protected by forest law – helped both to preserve game species and maintain the military prepared-ness of the country.

The origins of the word 'forest' are obscure. Whilst it may once have meant land covered with trees, for the Normans on mainland Europe the term was widely used to denote an area subject to special laws aimed at preserving wild game on behalf of the monarch. When the Normans invaded England they imported this notion with them and extended it further, to the extent that throughout the Middle Ages a forest was understood to be a place of deer, but not necessarily of trees.

In Manwood's *Lawes of the Forest*, published in 1598, the forest is defined as 'a certain territorie of woody grounds and fruitfull pastures, priviledged for wild beasts and foules of the forrest, chase and warren, to rest and abide in, in the safe protection of the king, for his princely delight and pleasure'. Furthermore, 'there should be woods in every Forest, both to shelter, and, at some times, to feed the Deer'. Yet while most forests indeed contained broad tracts of woodland, others encompassed large areas of open ground which included pastures and cultivated fields, even whole villages and towns. Many upland forests were composed principally of open moorland, such as the high parts of Exmoor Forest on the old red sandstone plateau of west Somerset and north Devon. By contrast, the Forest of Cornwall and of the Wirral in Cheshire were created simply by applying forest law to the ordinary countryside. Some of the most wooded areas in Britain – the Sussex Weald and north-west Warwickshire – contained few forests, while a number of moderately wooded counties, such as Wiltshire and Shropshire, contained many. Hampshire, one of the most densely afforested counties in England, contained the glittering jewel of the New Forest, one of William I's most significant creations.

Despite the reasons behind their creation, for much of their history most of the royal forests have not served primarily as hunting preserves for the king. A few later monarchs – among them Edward II – shared William I's passion for the chase, but the ordinary 'working' king had no time to visit the 80 or so royal forests, and records of royal hunts are surprisingly scarce. The monarch's hunting was carried out increasingly by trusted professionals, despatched to all parts of the country to secure the venison needed for feasts and holy days. The king's requirements were set out in great detail, as is clear from a royal command of the fourteenth century:

> 14th July, 1315. To the Sheriff of Somerset and Dorset. Order to pay to the King's yeomen, Robert Squier and David de Franketon, whom the King is sending with two berners, 24 running hounds, two veutrers, and nine greyhounds to take fat venison in the Forests of Rithiche, Pederton, Munedepe and Selewode, their wages while so engaged, to wit – 12d. a day each, 2d. a day for each of the berners, and 1½d. a day for each of the greyhounds. He is also to deliver to them salt and barrels for the venison and carriage for the same, and he is to put the venison in some certain place until further orders...

To the Warden of the Forest of Dertemore. Order to permit the
said Robert and David to take 20 stags. The like Orders to
the Wardens of the following Forests: Rithiche for 20 bucks,
Exmore for 20 stags, Pederton for 20 bucks, Selewode for 12
bucks, Munedepe for 12 bucks and 12 stags.

Although the king owned the deer in his forests, he was not necessarily the owner
of the land. In the Forest of Dean, for example, he owned the land and the trees,
but in Epping Forest the land was owned by nobles. His right to keep deer did
not give him absolute rights to the wood, the timber or the grazing. These rested
with the landowner or with commoners, those occupiers of particular farms and
cottages who held customary rights to such resources. Using the monarch's
prerogative for planting trees, Henry II extended the forest network by taking over
the land of neighbouring nobles and landowners. Not surprisingly, the earls and
barons objected to the king keeping his deer on their land, yet this unwelcome
sequestration of land continued during the reigns of Henry's sons, Richard I and
John, to the growing rage of the nobility. For the first time peers of the realm
found themselves in an ironic alliance with commoners, whose land rights had
been eroded by the application of forest law.

The despotic monarchy so united the people in opposition that in 1215 the royal
prerogative was finally curbed by Magna Carta, the Great Charter. Immediately
before Magna Carta there were at least 143 royal forests in England, the forest
serving as one of the king's greatest status symbols, a mark of his wealth and
power. It was a symbol keenly aspired to by nobles and by a handful of great
churchmen (already in Domesday the Earl of Chester is listed as owning three
forests, although at the time of John royal ownership amounted to more than
twice the number of forests held by all his subjects put together). However, after
Magna Carta no more royal forests were declared in England, although their
boundaries continued to be the subject of dispute.

Forest law
Offences against forest law fell into two categories – offences against *vert* and
those against venison. The first covered all those activities affecting the trees,
undergrowth and grassland within the forest, the aim being to protect the habitat
and food sources of the deer. Within a forest any freeholder felling trees, even if
within his own woods, or ploughing up his own pastures, was committing an
offence if he did not first obtain royal consent. He was considered guilty of *waste*,
and his land might be seized for the king's use until he had paid a fine. A freeholder
grubbing up trees by the roots was guilty of an offence known as assart, viewed as
especially serious since the act was deemed to completely destroy game cover.
The penalties for such offences provided foresters – the officers appointed to look
after forest game and timber – with great opportunities for extortion, and they
frequently abused their powers, bullying freeholders and commoners to make
payments to them, not just in money, but in hay, wheat, lambs or pigs.

In the Middle Ages mastiffs were bred specifically for the hunting of deer. This nineteenth-century portrait, by John Trivet Nettleship, is of 'Lion', the last in a long line of mastiffs reared at Lyme Park.

Offences against venison were devised for the specific protection of the deer themselves. Of all game animals, the stag was considered 'the king's beast', and anyone found harming one risked incurring the full weight of forest law. Even chasing a stag so as to cause it to pant could lead to imprisonment or to the offender being outlawed. When a deer was found dead or dying in the forest, an inquest would be held to establish how the animal had met its end. As part of these general protective measures, no greyhounds, mastiffs or other large dogs could be kept in the forest unless they had been 'lawed' or 'expeditated' – made lame by the removal of three claws from one forefoot. This would make them too slow to catch a deer. The 'lawing' of hounds caused much ill-feeling among forest dwellers, not for the cruelty involved, but because it was seen as an intrusion into domestic affairs.

Forest law was administered by three distinct courts. The lowest of these was the Woodmote or Forty Day Court, the function of which was to hold a preliminary inquiry. If the alleged offences appeared capable of being proven, they were passed on to the Swainmote or Court of Freeholders. The Swainmote could convict and impose fines in petty cases, but serious offences were committed to the highest court, the Justice Seat or Eyre of the forest. Meanwhile, the general management of the forest came under the overall authority of the keeper or warden, usually a person of high birth. In some forests, such as Savernake in Wiltshire, these important posts became hereditary. Below the warden were the verderers or judicial officers, responsible for the running of the forest courts and thereby the application of forest law. Below them, and on a more practical level, were the foresters, whose duty was to look after both the game and the timber; in this latter task they were assisted by the woodwards. The importance attached to the protection and management of timber is shown by the fact that every owner of woodland within the forest boundaries had to have a woodward.

Each forest was surveyed every three years, the survey being the responsibility of the regarders. They would report on any encroachments made on the forest, and carry out an examination of all hedges and fences. They were obliged to draw up lists of those local residents keeping hounds or in possession of bows and arrows, and also had to ensure that all mastiffs were lamed in accordance with forest law. Finally, grazing within the forest was overseen by the agisters, who were responsible for applying the rules dealing with rights of pasturage and for collecting the fees payable under these rights.

Forest law is often thought to have been applied with ruthless efficiency, with punishments of mutilation and even death being commonplace. The *Anglo-Saxon Chronicle* expressed the popular negative view of William the Conqueror's forest law:

> He made great protection for the game
> And imposed laws for the same
> That who so slew hart or hind
> Should be made blind…
> He preserved the harts and boars
> And loved stags as much
> As if he were their father.

Yet this view is disputed by some authorities, including landscape historian Oliver Rackham, who points out that there is little evidence to suggest such savagery. As he claims, perhaps forest courts were more interested in money than limbs. The theft of the king's deer might well mean imprisonment or a hefty fine in cases where the offenders were organised poachers or members of a large gang, but

Despite the unpopularity of forest law in some quarters, many forests and parks were in fact managed responsibly and with regard for the reciprocal rights between lord and commoner. During the eighteenth and nineteenth centuries nostalgia for this 'lost' sense of cooperative community spawned such bodies as the Ancient Order of Foresters – actually a friendly society and still thriving today.

ordinary individuals caught snaring a deer for the pot rarely came before the court, and when they did they were often pardoned. Meanwhile, 'trespasses against the vert' – usually damage caused to vegetation by the flouting of laws on grazing or wood-cutting – were punished by fines or the confiscation of livestock. Many of these fines amounted to no more than the value of the wood or the grazing involved, and it seems that the forest courts served more as a convenient means of collecting revenue than as a tool of brutal repression.

The working forest

While royal forests were designed mainly for the protection of deer – and for giving the monarch a monopoly over the valuable venison – they also provided a ready source of timber. Throughout the Middle Ages demand for timber was strong, and especially so for the construction of churches, barns and the houses of the nobility. Massive oak beams were required for roofs in particular, and the king took mature timber from his forests (he owned the timber in about half of them) for use in the construction of his own castles and palaces. Perhaps more significantly, he was able to use the gift of royal timber as a reward or inducement to his subjects. There are examples of timber serving as a particular tool of influence with religious orders, many of which were expanding their establishments at this time.

In medieval times forests and parks were very much working places. The sale of timber was a major source of income for many owners, including the crown, and large teams of woodcutters would have been employed felling and preparing this valuable commodity.

Although specimen trees destined for timber were allowed to grow to maturity, most trees were managed by either coppicing or pollarding. Most medieval woods were a mixture of coppice – the *silva minuta* of the Domesday Book and usually known as underwood – and larger, timber trees known as standards. Oaks were normally allowed to mature for about 70 years, or until they were ready to be felled and sawn or split into major timbers. Grazing animals such as cattle, pigs, sheep and goats were usually excluded from coppices by banks, ditches and hedges, in order to prevent the new shoots from being browsed. In areas of wood-pasture trees were managed by the system known in Domesday as *silva pastoralis*. This was a less intensive form of land use than coppicing. The broad sweeps

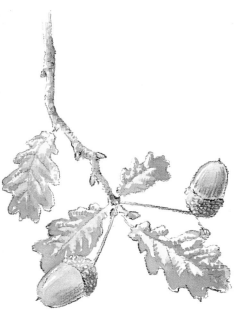

The pedunculate or English oak is perhaps the commonest parkland tree in Britain and can live for several centuries. In cultural terms the species has assumed almost iconic status and was traditionally celebrated on 29 May – Oak Apple Day.

of grassland – amounting to little more than extensive rough grazing – were interspersed with mature trees such as oak and beech, from which the acorns and mast provided a valuable autumn feed for pigs. The trees were either left to mature as standards or they were pollarded, the resulting poles growing out of the reach of grazing animals. This meant there was no need to enclose the area with hedges or ditches, and it was the practice of pollarding – combined with grazing – which maintained the wood-pasture landscape, with its open grasslands and scattered, individual trees.

Everyday life of the forest

Kings were not the only beneficiaries of the forest, despite its royal origin. While timber was chiefly the property of landowners, commoners enjoyed extensive rights to graze their livestock on the wooded pastures and to harvest poles from the pollarded trees. While forest law protected the king's venison, customary rights allowed ordinary citizens to pasture their cattle on forest grazings and gather wood for their fences and fires. It was these very activities which created and preserved the landscape of wood-pasture. In many forests commoners enjoyed rights of *hedgebote* – the taking of wood for fencing. Perhaps more

Saddleback pigs at pannage, now an unusual sight in Britain. Perhaps only in the New Forest does the practice continue with any regularity.

valuable, however, was the right to *firebote* – the collection of underwood, usually dead-wood, for domestic fuel, an entitlement often extended to religious houses. In Wiltshire the nuns of Wilton were allowed four score loads of firewood from Melchet Forest, while the nuns of Amesbury were entitled to fifteen *robora* – dead trees and the stumps, or bollings, of pollards – from local forests for their fire.

The right to graze cattle and horses applied to forest pastures just as it did to a conventional common, and by the thirteenth century the terms were being strictly defined in a bid to prevent overuse. Unless the wood-pasture was entirely common, the owner would usually collect a small fee in cash or kind for each beast pastured, and so grazing was usually confined to fixed numbers of livestock and for specified periods of the year. For example, in 1227 each of the tenants of Escrick in Yorkshire were permitted to graze ten cattle, ten pigs and a score of sheep in the manorial woodland. Heavy demand meant that a degree of refined administration was called for, and by the late Middle Ages grazing rights were usually subdivided into three categories: agistment was the right to pasture cattle, which were often left out for much of the year because of the shelter afforded by trees; pannage allowed an individual to run his or her pigs in a wood to forage for oak and beech mast in the autumn, and finally, the right – often claimed by the inhabitants of ancient houses in wood-pasture areas – to run their cows, bullocks and horses in the wood. In many instances, such as in Rockingham Forest, Leicestershire, it was argued that this right was in partial recompense for the full – and often damaging – access allowed under forest law for deer to graze on the villagers' lands. The value to local villagers of grazing and other rights in forests was, apparently, still significant into the nineteeth century; William Cobbett noted how ordinary folk in wooded areas suffered less from poverty than their brethren in purely agricultural districts. Nor was it just local people who could benefit from such rights; it was often possible for outsiders to buy agistments to run their stock in a forest.

One important custom was that by which all livestock had to be removed from the forest for the duration of the fence month, a period lasting from a fortnight before midsummer to St Cyril's Day, fifteen days after midsummer. This was the month of fawning, and the forests were maintained as places for the 'quiet and preservation of wild beasts'. The term 'fence' came from *defence*, namely the defence of deer from disturbance. The custom seems to have dated back to the time of Canute, but the Norman kings applied it with rigour. Pannage was not allowed at this time, and nor were the gathering of rushes or the cutting of wood.

Although no new dwellings were permitted in a forest (it was considered that any increase in population was likely to disturb the deer), there was a custom allowing a squatter to put up a house overnight. Provided he was able to get his fire lit before morning, he not only secured the right to remain there permanently, but also enjoyed the usual common rights such as pasturage and turbary, the cutting of turf. These rights appear to have been attached only to the original chimney and hearth, so that if a house were later to be enlarged or rebuilt, these would need to be retained for the rights to continue.

Forest legends
Stories of the brutality shown by Norman kings in the preservation of their forests (and the deer therein) passed down the generations to help create a powerful mythology of oppression. Tales of savage punishments meted out to those who contravened forest law caught the popular imagination. Obscure medieval statutes setting out barbaric penalties for offenders appeared to add historic weight to the mythology.

Rufus, son of William the Conqueror, became the chief villain, inheriting both his father's passion for hunting and his contempt for the common rights of grazing and gathering wood. It was claimed that, as the royal forests were extended, entire parishes disappeared, victims of the Norman tyranny, and the death of Rufus in 1100 by an arrow 'intended' for a deer was widely seen as divine retribution for the wrongs he had perpetrated against the forest dwellers. Indeed, the whole dynasty of the Conqueror seems to have been cursed for their crimes against the freedom of the 'greenwood'; another of William's sons, Richard, was

An enduring landscape

This illustration from James Doyle's 1864 *Chronicle of England* shows the slaying of William II whilst hunting deer in the New Forest. His assassin was never caught.

killed in the New Forest, as was his grandson. The legend of Norman despots demolishing whole villages and parishes to create a private hunting reserve in the New Forest was further fuelled by claims made by medieval clerics such as Oderic and Walter Map, archdeacon of Oxford. Their contentions passed into popular culture, and produced the mythic memory of the greenwood as the battleground of England's early struggle for freedom. According to landscape historian Simon Schama, the hunt was 'an alien despotism, the hoofs of its horses trampling primitive liberties embodied, it was said, in the Saxon assembly, the *witengamot*, or the Scottish midsummer assembly at Glen Taner, where tribal chiefs met in their clan games'.

Out of such popular sentiments arose the legend of Robin Hood, the great cultural icon marking out the greenwood as the natural *locus* of the people's desire for freedom. His enemies were not the king but an army of ruthless and self-serving office-holders, including sheriffs, foresters, corrupt clerics and encroachers. According to Schama, the greenwood of Robin Hood 'is an elegy for a world of liberty and justice that had never existed: one where the relation between leader and led is of unsullied reciprocity and where the purest form of fellowship is the open-air forest feast'.

So in the memory of the British the medieval forest has become a rural idyll, a sylvan setting in which greed and corruption have no place and where justice and decency hold sway. Before the coming of the Norman tyrant, goes the legend, lord and peasant, thane and churl, lived side-by-side, each respectful of the interests and rights of the other. In this ancient woodland community the leaves were ever green and the bright sunlight fell in shafts upon the grassy glade. Yet the real situation was somewhat different. By Saxon times the wooded areas of Britain had already become the site of conflicting economic and social interests, with much ancient woodland swept away to make way for cultivated fields and pasturelands. In those afforested stretches that did remain, conversion to arable land, pasture and orchard was often proceeding apace. By placing hunting firmly at the heart of their martial culture, the Norman monarchs arrested the decline in the status and role of the forest. No doubt the impact of their system of administration on working woodland communities could be traumatic, but the actions of the Norman kings did help maintain the woodland habitats and the ancient landscape of wood-pasture contained therein.

Wood-pastures – private and public

In medieval England wood-pasture was not restricted to the royal forest. Outside the forests lay extensive areas of private forest known as chases, usually created when the owner of a chase – most often a noble or a senior cleric – was granted hunting rights by the king. Like the true forests, chases frequently included areas of wood-pasture, as well as woodland, and in the Middle Ages the terms 'chase' and 'forest' were synonymous. There was, however, one important difference: while the royal forest was subject to forest law, the private chase was normally governed by common law.

Wood-pasture was also found in areas of enclosed forest or woodland known as 'parks'. Although a few parks had existed before the Conquest, they were largely an innovation of the Normans, who developed them as a form of game larder. Enclosed by ditches and banks, on the top of which was the pale (effectively a wooden fence), these parks were particularly well-suited to the holding of fallow deer. It was the Norman deer park that was to metamorphose, firstly into the landscape park of the eighteenth century, and then into the modern urban park, thereby providing a cultural link with the primeval forest.

There was another important progenitor of parkland in medieval Britain: the wood-pasture common. According to Rackham, the typical wood-pasture common was dominated by grassland or heather with a scattering of trees and

A mighty former beech pollard at Frithsden on the National Trust's Ashridge Estate. Such trees are remnants of the wood-pasture that once existed here.

bushes of varying density. The grass was grazed by a variety of livestock ranging from horses to geese, and, as in the deer parks, trees were normally pollarded to prevent grazing livestock or deer from browsing on the regrowths. From the earliest times wood-pasture commons had been used by a large section of the village community, rather than by a few nobles, and while the deer park and chase were essentially private domains, these wood-pastures were mostly used and managed communally. Like other areas of common they belonged to a landowner, usually the lord of the manor, but the rights to use them were held by those commoners occupying particular properties. In this sense wood-pasture common was very much a public amenity. Typically the grazing belonged to the commoners, with ownership of the soil – including mineral rights – retained by the owner. The trees might be owned by either party, with the timber often remaining the property of the landowner and the commoners holding rights to the wood (both the underwood and the poles from pollards). These common rights were administered by the manorial courts, usually composed of the commoners themselves.

However, through the centuries the practices which were essential for the maintenance of wood-pasture gradually fell from use. The crown's interest in forests began to wane after the reign of Henry III (died 1272). At first many were run as ordinary commons, with the ancient forest courts being retained to administer the commoners' rights to grazing and wood. Meanwhile, wood-pasture commons proved particularly vulnerable to changed land management practices, their destruction often being brought about by a reduction in grazing, with shrubs and trees growing up on the former pasture and leading ultimately to closed-canopy woodland. The Mens, an ancient wooded common in Sussex, still bears many characteristics of an uncultivated Saxon landscape – except that the pastures have reverted to new woodland. Today a few mighty pollards, most of them engulfed in younger trees, are the only indication that in the Middle Ages this was a thriving wood-pasture landscape. Equally, the former wood-pasture common of Frithsden Beeches in Hertfordshire has been virtually swallowed up by secondary woodland, the collection of fine old pollard beeches hidden within serving to remind us of a richer past.

Many wood-pasture commons fell victim to the enclosure movement of the late eighteenth century. Most vulnerable were the larger commons, those most likely to have trees. The Enclosure Acts often gave landowners the power to curtail common rights and do what they pleased with the wood-pasture. All too often they destroyed it, felling the older trees for their timber and turning the land over to full-scale agriculture, a more profitable option (at least during periods of rising population).

In more recent times the advance of modern forestry caused the replacement of the old, gnarled pollards with serried rows of plantation trees. Of the great forests that were once abundant in Britain, sadly none now survives in anything other

An enduring landscape

Moccas Park is still surrounded by a wooden deer pale of a type once common around parks across England and Wales.

than fragmented form. Rackham tells the poignant story of the majestic Forest of Dean, with its 'rich history of pastures, coppices and outsize timber trees, of deer and wild swine, roadside trenches, and industries going back to the Romans'. It is a history now largely obliterated. Today the area is 'blanketed with plantations of uniform, poorly-grown oaks whose later replacement, in part, by conifers is hardly to be regretted'.

Of the wood-pastures that do survive, those areas within the New Forest in Hampshire are considered collectively to be the largest survival of this type of landscape in western Europe. Over the centuries a sophisticated system for controlling the use of common lands in the New Forest was operated by the steward, his statutory role now assumed by the New Forest Verderers, who regulate the exercise of common rights. In this way the ancient wood-pasture landscape continues to be protected. Although on a smaller scale, Hatfield Forest is even better preserved, with its ancient coppice woodlands, open, grassy 'plains' and broad stretches of wood-pasture containing hundreds of old pollards.

Like the forests, deer parks also began a long, slow decline following their heyday at the opening of the fourteenth century. At a time of rising wages – a result of the population collapse caused by the Black Death in 1348 – landowners found it increasingly difficult to justify the luxury of a park-keeper for such an unprofitable use of land. Today few medieval parks survive in 'working order'. Two notable exceptions are Moccas Park in Herefordshire, where venerable oaks and ashes continue to brood over pastures on which fallow deer, sheep and cattle graze, and Staverton Park in Suffolk, which still contains 4000 pollard oaks and an assembly of massive hollies, birches and rowans.

The precise total area of Britain's remaining wood-pasture is difficult to calculate. There are no reliable estimates of the current extent of parkland or other forms of lowland wood-pasture, although the total is unlikely to exceed 30,000 hectares. In the uplands the area of oak-dominated wood-pasture may amount to double this figure. Whatever the true total, Britain's remaining stock of wood-pasture landscape is small. Yet its survival is vital, and most wood-pastures are worth preserving simply as attractive areas of countryside. Their real value lies perhaps more in their embodiment of many of the social, political and economic elements that went into the making of a nation.

There is another, equally compelling, reason for protecting what remains of Britain's unique wood-pasture heritage. In Windsor Great Park – on the very edge of a huge urban conurbation – it is still possible to view an ancient forest landscape, complete with red deer. The park contains the largest and most important assemblage of ancient trees in the whole of western Europe, and is one of the few places in Britain to have supported a continuous succession of old trees dating back as far as the original wildwood. The oldest oaks – 'those spectacular living shells with dead tops and billows of foliage' – are reputed to be

An enduring landscape

up to 800 years old. A single massive tree close to Forest Lodge, 'its cavernous bolling held together by iron pins and braces, its boughs propped up with crutches', may even pre-date the establishment of Windsor Forest by William the Conqueror shortly after 1066. Many such veterans began life as working trees, being regularly lopped or pollarded to provide wood for fuel, fencing and construction materials. They now provide us with a living cultural link to human activities that are fast fading into history.

As the location of many of Britain's dwindling number of ancient trees, wood-pasture is also important as a reservoir for many different forms of wildlife, providing habitat for scores of invertebrates, fungi and lichens, particularly those that need dead-wood to survive. The ecology of old forest areas is closely related to that of the primeval forest that once covered Britain, and to the ecology of the first wood-pastures. However, for the past 500 years or so the story of wood-pasture and the creatures that depend on it has not been limited to the survival of segments of royal forests. It has equally been the story of parks.

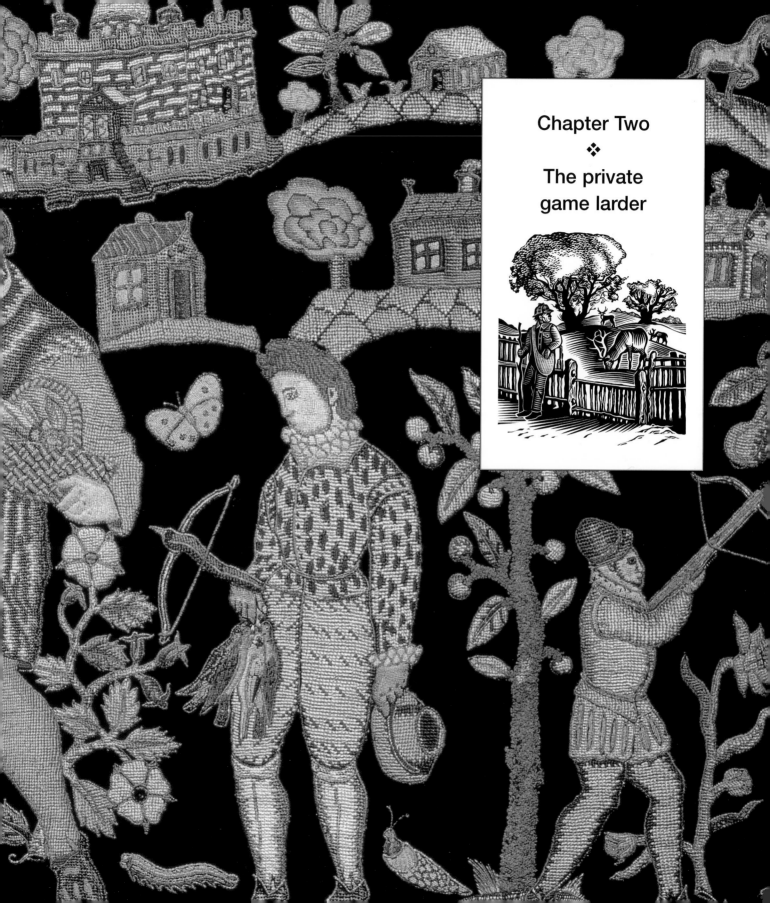

Chapter Two

❖

The private game larder

THE PRIVATE GAME LARDER

Norman culture had created a profound disruption in the daily life of village England. William I soon stripped the Saxon thanes and lords of their land and bestowed it on his closest followers, an elite of 170 nobles. In return for the gift of these estates, the new tenants-in-chief were required to provide a fixed number of armoured, mounted knights-at-arms, all of them ready to take to the field at a moment's notice. The knights served as a professional warrior cadre, acting as the iron fist of the king and enforcing the stern martial culture and code of honour for which the Normans were renowned and feared. Their presence and influence was to have a considerable bearing on England's landscape, and was the driving force behind the widespread introduction of the fallow deer and the proliferation of deer parks that followed. These parks were the precursors, both in terms of theory and practice, of the private sporting estates for which England in particular was to become celebrated in later centuries.

The king's beast

Primarily a native of southern Europe, the status of the fallow deer as an indigenous or introduced species in Britain has long been in doubt. Archaeological deposits reveal its probable presence here during the last interglacial period of the Upper Pleistocene (some 150,000 years ago) but it then appears to have died out, only to be reintroduced – probably by Phoenician traders – during the Bronze or Iron Ages. It was certainly established in England by Roman times, and was hunted by Saxon lords before the Norman Conquest. It was the Normans, however, who set about introducing the species extensively across lowland England, and during the late eleventh century considerable numbers were released into English forests.

The Normans realised that by confining the great herds of fallow deer within wooden fences or pales they could increase by ten-fold the production of venison

Regarded as the most appropriate sport for royalty, the hunting of deer had powerful connotations and appears regularly in medieval imagery, as in this thirteenth-century illustration.

(previous spread) To the hunter, parks could yield a rich bounty. This embroidery of the *Fancie of the Fowler*, from a late Elizabethan cushion cover at Hardwick Hall in Derbyshire, shows a huntsman returning to his family after a productive foray.

from a given area of land. The fallow had the advantage of being a gregarious species, less aggressive in the rut than the red and roe deer, and generally content to graze alongside cattle and horses. It was therefore supremely well-suited to this early form of intensive livestock husbandry. At great cost the Norman landholders enclosed sections of forest behind a combination of earth bank, pale and ditch. These were essentially private stores of meat and timber, places where a powerful social elite could garner and secure natural products.

When William's conquering army crossed the Channel, parks were not unknown in England. The oldest recorded English park – Ongar Great Park in Essex – is mentioned in an Anglo-Saxon will containing the word *deerhag*, an enclosure for deer. Dyrham Park in South Gloucestershire takes its name from the Anglo-Saxon *deor-hamm*, another term for deer enclosure. Clearly at least a handful of deer parks probably predated the Norman Conquest, but what is beyond dispute is that under the Normans the number of deer parks increased by leaps and bounds. The Domesday Book refers to 31, and according to one estimate by the year 1300 the number exceeded 3000, representing up to two per cent of the land area of England.

The generally docile nature and variable pelage of fallow deer made them an ideal species with which the Normans could stock their parks.

Once the capital of Deheubarth, one of the three ancient kingdoms of Wales, Dinefwr Castle is now in ruins but still sits in a magnificent park, grazed by sheep, fallow deer and the famous white cattle.

Settled areas with fertile soils were generally considered by the imparkers to be unsuitable for deer and hunting, as they required too much change to the landscape (most notably the planting of trees). But wooded counties – especially those freed from the restrictions of forest law – were well suited to the creation of parks, and deer parks were therefore most numerous in well-wooded counties such as Hampshire, Essex, Staffordshire, Worcestershire, Warwickshire and Hertfordshire, the most densely 'parked' county of all and which was said to have had a park to every seven square miles. Far fewer parks were created in Wales, and most examples were sited near the border with England. One notable exception is the magnificent park at Dinefwr in Carmarthenshire, where in the tenth century the local Princes of Deheubarth received their obligations in white park cattle. The latter continued to roam the park until the 1970s, and have now been re-established by the National Trust.

The first parks were owned by the king, his nobles and senior members of the clergy. Of the parks mentioned in the Domesday Book, eight belonged to William I and six to leading churchmen. Henry II built his palace in the vast Anglo-Saxon deer park at Woodstock in Oxfordshire, while the great park at Clarendon in Wiltshire was the setting for Henry III's palace. However, park ownership did cascade down the social scale so that by the fourteenth century most earls and bishops could afford a handful of them, and even the minor gentry could aspire to one or two.

Since the monarch claimed ownership of all deer and 'other beasts of the chase' – fiercely protected under forest law – landholders were required to obtain royal consent before they could enclose a park. From the thirteenth century this permission took the form of a 'licence to empark', with every application triggering a land search. This was designed to ensure that the king's interests would not be harmed by the granting of a licence. Despite such obstacles, medieval nobles clamoured to set up deer parks of their own. While hunting within the pale rarely provided the excitement of the chase through the open forest – where mounted huntsmen, their servants and hounds might pursue a stag for several miles – the possession of a private hunting ground certainly conferred prestige and status on its owner. However, the principal purpose of the deer park was actually to supply food. Within the confines of a pale deer could be bred and reared more efficiently than in the open forest, and could certainly be killed more conveniently.

Venison was no ordinary meat. In the martial culture of the early Middle Ages all meats were prized, as they were believed to promote virility and strength. However, the meats of the fallow and red deer were the most highly regarded, being reserved for feasts and the honouring of guests. Since Saxon times venison had been regarded as a prestigious part of the aristocratic diet, a mark of high social status, and in the Middle Ages it was regularly packed in barrels, salted, and sent to the king or to other feudal magnates, sometimes over long distances. While hunting as a sport took place in parks from time to time, regular culling of deer was carried out by professional servants charged with the task of supplying their employers with venison whenever it was required. In 1248 the keeper of Newton Park in Somerset received an order to allow the king's huntsmen to take five stags for salting and dispatch to Winchester in time for Whitsuntide.

Although the creators of England's first parks were motivated chiefly by their relish for venison, they were not without an aesthetic appreciation of managed nature. They had seen it elsewhere in Europe. Columella, the first-century Roman writer on agriculture, describes similar park-like enclosures in Italy and Gaul, their owners often siting them in places where they could be seen and admired as an attractive landscape. Norman nobles would have seen parks during their conquest of Sicily, where deer and hunting enclosures had been established by the Arabs. They were described in the twelfth century by Archbishop Romuald of Salerno:

> And certain hills and forests around Palermo likewise enclosed with walls, and there he made the Parco – a pleasant and delightful spot, shaded with various trees and abounding with deer and goats and wild boar. And here he also raised a palace, to which the water was led in underground pipes from springs from whence it flowed ever sweet and clear... In the winter and in Lent he would reside at Favara, by reason of the great quantity of fish that were to be had there; while in the heat of summer he would find solace at the Parco where with a little hunting, he would relieve his mind from the cares and worries of state.

No doubt the Norman park creators gained the same sense of spiritual refreshment from the enclaves of wood-pasture they carved out from the woods and wastes that made up most of lowland Britain. But their primary purposes remained the production of meat and the provision of land for their own recreation. It was not until Tudor times that the idea of the park as ornament gained widespread currency.

The management of deer

The owners of most medieval deer parks employed a parker to look after the deer and take charge of the day-to-day management. The post was highly sought after, especially by the younger sons of noblemen, who were left without a livelihood by the law of primogeniture – the absolute right of succession of the eldest son. The parker was usually provided with a lodge within the park pale, from where he could keep a close eye on his stock. He was expected to be constantly vigilant, taking a daily turn around the park and maintaining a detailed record of deer numbers. Keeping track of deer was not always easy, even within the pale. The best parkland included a variety of vegetation and landscape types, among them smooth, turfed 'launds', rough grazing, woodlands containing a proportion of underwood, hawthorn-covered banks and bramble-strewn thickets. Especially important were the bracken-covered brakes in which does and fawns might lie up. Woody glades were also considered essential. Here the deer might find shelter during harsh winter weather, and the glades also provided convenient places for putting out supplementary rations of beans and hay whenever frost and snow limited natural food sources. Some parkers put up sheds to provide their herds with winter shelter, but most thought such artificial expedients damaging to the hardiness of such 'wild beasts'.

A characteristic feature of the medieval deer park were its pollarded trees – often ancient oaks – scattered across the grass launds. Trees provided the framework for long, uninterrupted vistas which were to become the quintessential image of parkland. It was an image seized upon by eighteenth-century park designers in creating an idealised landscape that would prove to be enduringly English. On the attributes of a successful deer park the nineteenth-century writer Evelyn Shirley quoted the Earl of Winchilsea, owner of Eastwell Park in Kent:

> The true secret of a good park consists in a good original stock; soil not too rich, but various, with a short bite in most places; a well kept-up succession of deer, so that none should be killed too early, or left until too late; quiet, shelter, and a good keeper, the last, not least; for whoever saw a good herd of deer under the management of any man that not only did not thoroughly understand but take pleasure in his business.

The size and majesty of a red deer stag made it a highly prized quarry for the hunt. The erratic distribution of red deer in Britain directly reflects their history as an introduced parkland species.

41

At most deer parks the perimeter pale was interrupted by entry gates and also by a deer leap or saltatorium, a device allowing deer to jump into an enclosed area but not out again. Deer leaps took a variety of forms. For example, a leap might be a simple earth ramp leading to the top of the wall, or the pale might be reduced in height at a point where the interior ditch was widened and made deeper. A licence to construct a saltatorium had to be sought from the king, who laid claim to all the nation's deer; such a licence was granted in 1324 to the Bishop of Bath and Wells, who was allowed two deer leaps in each of his parks at Evercreech and Wellington in Somerset, both of them outside royal forests. Permission was rarely granted for private parks located inside, or even near, a royal forest.

Deer leaps were a common feature of most parks and were part of an increasingly elaborate system of deer management.

The presence of the parker in his lodge within the park pale was intended to deter poachers, although in practice it seldom did. The author of a French treatise on deer parks gives clear instructions for the defence of the lodge against any malicious intruders, the keeper being encouraged to defend himself by 'shooting

with his bowes, casting stones or scalding water, to make them avoid from the same'. How often English park-keepers were required to take such drastic measures is hard to guess. In any case it seems to have been of little avail, as throughout the Middle Ages poaching was a regular pursuit of the poor and underprivileged, particularly in the relatively unpopulated parts of the country where deer parks were most abundant.

In many cases poaching arose from sheer necessity. By the fourteenth century ordinary people had been excluded from any form of hunting by game laws, and only those with property worth at least 40 shillings a year – a considerable sum in the Middle Ages – were permitted to keep greyhounds and ferrets, or to use nets or other means of taking deer, hares and rabbits. Denied any lawful means of taking game, many people opted to steal it. Medieval manorial courts were kept busy dealing with a steady stream of cases involving park-breaking (a breach of the law could be punished by a year's imprisonment), with frequent instances of deer being pursued by intruders with greyhounds and bows and arrows. Most offences concerned single deer taken by individuals or small groups of family and friends, but occasionally large-scale poaching would become the object of organised crime. During the thirteenth century at Gannow in Worcestershire a band of up to one hundred fugitives, led by one Geoffrey du Park, were said to dine regularly on venison stolen from Feckenham Forest and local deer parks.

A diversity of products

For the lawless, poor or destitute, there was much in the deer park to tempt them. Parks were extremely productive, and as the centuries passed they became even more so, as their owners became more efficient managers of the resources contained therein. For example, a single park of 445 hectares produced an average cull of 44 fallow deer annually in the years 1234–63, the same yield as an area of unenclosed royal forest ten times larger. While deer were becoming ever more scarce in the open forest, they were conveniently multiplying within the confines of the pale.

There was also a variety of other meat available. The term 'warren' originally referred to the right of the local lord to hunt for certain small game on his estate, which included quarry such as badgers, foxes, rabbits, pigeons, pheasants, partridges and plovers, with the principal beast of the warren being the hare. After a time, however, warren came to imply solely rabbits, which had been introduced to England by the Normans early in the twelfth century. The first warrens were established on islands, such as the Scillies, Lundy and the Farnes. Rabbits became highly prized in the Middle Ages for their flesh and their fur, both of which were traded extensively, and by the mid-thirteenth century warrens were being established at a variety of sites on the British mainland. They were particularly frequent inside deer parks, where the animals could be afforded greater security from poachers. Inside parks they were kept in small enclosures known as coningers, surrounded by earthworks and fencing.

Parks served as venues for the hunting of a variety of beasts. Whilst rabbits were raised in warrens for their meat and fur, hares were decidedly wild game and avidly pursued on horseback and with dogs.

The medieval rabbit was a delicate animal of Mediterranean origin, ill-suited to the harsh British climate. It had to be protected from predators and encouraged to burrow in the ground. To assist it park-keepers constructed special earthworks in the form of rectangular, flat-topped mounds bounded by shallow ditches. These 'pillow mounds' were made in a variety of sizes and frequently arranged in groups of up to 80 or more, which were often linked together in complex patterns such as squares and crosses. The aim was not merely to provide the animals with a suitable home, but to retain them in structures that would be simple to harvest using nets and ferrets. The ditches surrounding the mounds were dug down to the harder subsoil, which prevented the rabbits from creating a rambling network of tunnels through which they might escape the warrener and his ferrets.

Because of their greater security, deer parks were also favoured places for the rearing of table fish in ponds. At their simplest these were made by constructing an earth bank across a stream to form a dam; unless the valley sides were steep, two additional embankments were built parallel to the line of the watercourse. Fishponds came in a variety of forms and sizes, but medieval writers usually distinguished between the larger breeding ponds, known as *vivaria* or 'great waters', and the smaller *servatoria* or 'stewponds' in which fish were held ready for consumption. Some of the larger parks contained fishponds of considerable complexity, with separate tanks for breeding, rearing, fattening and storage. A particularly lavish example was built in 1169 at the royal manor of Feckenham in Worcestershire. It was repaired and enlarged in 1204 at the exorbitant cost of £40 and later outlays on its maintenance can be traced in the royal accounts.

Moats were also used for holding fish, and many examples exist of landowners stocking their moats with various species. Pike and bream were the popular fish of the early Middle Ages, and in 1250 Henry III – temporarily holding the manor of Taunton following the death of Bishop Peter des Roches – ordered 40 bream and ten pike from ponds in its park for the Christmas feast at Winchester. However, eels, tench, perch and roach also feature regularly in contemporary records, although by the fourteenth century the faster-growing and hardier carp had replaced most other species in the stewponds of English parks.

Being able to serve fish at table, or make gifts of fish to others, was very much a mark of wealth and status. This led many park-owners to establish fishponds in which species such as carp (foreground) could be reared successfully, although smaller varieties such as roach (behind) remained important.

The private game larder

The farming of pigeons was also a feature of medieval parks. Like fish ponds, dovecotes or 'culver-houses' were often sited close to the main house for both convenience and greater security. Pigeons provided a year-round source of protein, each female producing a pair of chicks up to ten times a year. The young birds or squabs were usually culled at four weeks, before the pin feathers had developed and while they were still covered in down. At this age the flesh was deemed to be at its most tender and succulent. Some of the larger dovecotes contained up to several hundred nest holes and were substantial structures, an indication of their importance both in terms of supplying fresh meat and conferring status on their owner. Considerable effort was invested in their construction and maintenance: in the larger circular dovecotes for example, the squabs were harvested by means of a potence, a revolving stairway mounted on a central pivot. One of these can still be seen at the National Trust's Kinwarton Dovecote in Warwickshire.

In the seventeenth century the owners of deer parks containing lakes and other areas of open water introduced a new game-producing enterprise, one more akin to hunting than farming. It involved the capture of wildfowl by means of a device called a decoy, an idea introduced to England from Holland. Park owners would construct curved 'pipes', long covered channels made from netting supported on a framework of hoops. Built on an area of open water, each pipe was wide at the mouth, gradually tapering to a narrow point at which a large bow-net was attached. One or both sides of the pipe would be screened by reeds, behind which the decoy operator would hide himself. A flock of wild ducks landing on

Any self-respecting estate would have a dovecote and stewpond. At Cotehele in Cornwall these date back to medieval times and would have supplied the adjacent house with a plentiful supply of meat and fish.

Dovecotes were subject to considerable architectural pretension. This 1555 example shows the birds living in a castellated affair several storeys high.

the water would then be lured into the mouth of the pipe by tame decoy ducks. Sometimes a small dog would be trained to act as a 'piper' and low boards or 'dog jumps' built behind the reed screen provided hidden platforms for the piper to jump up and down on. For some reason the sight of a dog continuously appearing and disappearing behind the reeds acted as an irresistible lure to the wildfowl gathered at the mouth of the pipe. The dog – together with the decoy ducks – induced the birds to swim a little way inside the pipe. The operator would then jump out from his reed hide, and by shouting and waving his arms scare the birds into flight down the tapering pipe and into the net at the end. There they would be killed.

In 1722 Daniel Defoe wrote of the impressive harvest of the decoys he had seen in Cambridgeshire:

> In these fens are an abundance of those admirable pieces of art called duckoys… places so adapted for the harbour and shelter of wild-fowl, and then furnished with a breed of those they call decoy-ducks, who are taught to allure and entice their kind to the places they belong to, that it is incredible what quantities of wild-fowl of all sorts, duck, mallard, teal, widgeon &c. they take in those duckoys every week during the season.

Decoys became quite common in parks containing suitable stretches of water which could be adapted. The ducks killed were a valuable source of food in winter, and some decoys continued in use into the early years of the twentieth century. That at Boarstall in Buckinghamshire, dating from the late seventeenth century and now in the care of the National Trust, is still operational – the birds trapped are ringed for scientific purposes and then released.

Landscape historian Tom Williamson has described the various animal enterprises in parks as 'intermediate forms of exploitation', forms of management that were neither the hunting of wild species nor the husbandry of domestic breeds, but something in between. These enterprises enjoyed their heyday during the period between the mid-seventeenth and the mid-eighteenth centuries, whereafter estate owners became more interested in running conventional agricultural enterprises.

Of course there had always been other, more prosaic, products of the deer park. Sheep and cattle were frequently grazed within the pale, often mixing freely with deer. Park owners could earn a sizeable cash income from agistments (see p.24), and some parks even contained areas of arable land, although growing crops was clearly incompatible with free-roaming deer. Parks were also used as breeding places for horses. So vital was the horse for transportation and military purposes that in 1536 Henry VIII had passed an act encouraging park owners to

One of the very few British duck decoys still in working order is that at Boarstall near Aylesbury. For over 250 years it supplied wildfowl to the estate kitchen, with a record annual catch of 2500 birds. Regular decoying stopped in 1939/40, but has since been revived.

set up studs. The act was revived during Elizabeth I's reign, when those with 'inclosed grounds' were obliged to keep mares for breeding, the number determined by the park's area. It was decreed that 'every man that hath a park of his own, or in lease or in keeping for term of life of the compass of one mile, shall keep in the same two mares, and every man that shall have a park of the compass of four miles, shall keep four mares… every man that hath a park of the compass of two miles and upwards to four miles, shall keep three mares'.

As well as producing meat and animals, the deer park grew steadily in importance as a source of timber and wood. Outside the parks many of Britain's woodlands were coming under intensive management by coppicing. Only under the wood-pasture regime of the park was it possible to find the mature standard trees sought by the builders of large houses, churches and chapels. The variety and amounts supplied could be prodigious: for example, over a 48 year period in the mid-thirteenth century Newton Park in Somerset supplied cruck blades to Godfrey de Crocombe for the building of a barn, 70 oaks to the sisters of the Order of St John for the rebuilding of their house in Minchin Buckland, eighteen oaks to the Blackfriars of Ilchester, three oaks to the people of Somerton for the repair of their belfry, and five oaks to the Greyfriars of Bridgwater towards the

building of their dormitory. Timber was also supplied for fine woodworking at Cleeve Abbey and at the abbey church at Glastonbury. In addition, dead trees, wind-fallen wood and undergrowth were supplied as fuel. In some parks wooded areas could be separated from the launds or grazing areas and turned into coppices, producing poles for fencing and construction, together with underwood for fuel. In open, 'uncompartmented' parks, pollards continued as the main providers of a regular harvest of wood and poles.

For six centuries or more the deer park acted as a kind of farm, producing an ever greater diversity of products. Yet these 'farms' were owned by a tiny social elite, and the meats raised within them were generally denied to the common people. From their very inception deer parks were symbols of power, privilege and prestige. So were the animals, fish and fowl reared inside them, most game animals remaining the preserve of the wealthy; as late as 1671 the Game Act stipulated that hares, rabbits and game birds could be taken only by those possessing freehold property worth at least £100 a year or copyholds worth at least £150 a year. The private park stocked with deer and the trappings of production was most decidedly the mark of a gentleman and of someone wealthy enough to enjoy a variety of scarce and exotic foods at a time when the fear of hunger still stalked the common people.

Such exclusivity of access conferred both practical and strategic advantages: it allowed the gentry to bestow gifts of game and fish on their neighbours and friends, or on staff and servants in recognition of loyal service. The symbolism of such largesse was huge: a pair of pigeons or a haunch of venison were potent reminders to the community of the wealth and status of the giver, serving to help maintain and reinforce the existing social order.

Quite understandably, parks bred resentment on the part of those denied access to their benefits. For many ordinary villagers the park enterprise which created most annoyance was often the dovecote. Ownership of a dovecote was the strict prerogative of the lord of the manor, yet the pigeons that lived in it fed on all the crops of the surrounding countryside, those of lord and commoner alike. The gentry therefore enjoyed an exclusive form of protein whose production costs were borne by the whole community: an obvious potential source of discord. For example, during the English Civil War – and the years following – structures such as pigeon houses and fishponds became obvious targets for Parliamentary forces filled with revolutionary zeal. What more powerful symbols of unjust privilege and injustice than the tall, ornate dovecote and the park containing it?

A playground for the wealthy

For all its intense productivity, the deer park remained the place where the gentry went for recreation. And their favourite form of recreation remained the hunt, although it was a very different style of hunting from that favoured by the monarch and his nobles in the open forest. The Norman kings and nobles had

Large trees from forests and parks were regularly felled to meet the demand for timber. The fourteenth-century tithe barn at Lacock in Wiltshire, built to store the rent and dues paid in kind – as corn, hides and fleeces – to the nearby abbey, is typical of the large ecclesiastical buildings of the period.

The private game larder

A full hunt was a sizeable affair, with many helpers and followers. This nineteenth-century illustration gives a rather fanciful idea of thirteenth-century hunting attire and equipment.

enjoyed 'hunting at force' with mounted horsemen, their servants and hounds pursuing a stag for miles through the royal forest or private chase. The English longbow was their weapon of choice. The hunt or 'chase' (Fr. *chasse*) was invested with much solemnity and respect by the Norman knights. It was an opportunity to display courage, endurance, discipline and horsemanship, along with which went a spirit of courtesy and fair play. Quarry had to be taken with 'nobleness and gentleness… and not killed falsely'. Falseness was regarded as a character weakness associated with the lower orders of society, while the chivalrous spirit was a virtue of the upper classes.

While the ethics of the chase were often applied to the enclosed arena of the park, the method of hunting changed markedly. The new style hunt marked something of a return to the methods used in Saxon times, when huntsmen possessed neither the horses suited for a long chase nor the weaponry needed

to bring down a deer at distance. In the pre-Norman forest a labyrinth of alleys would be cut at some convenient spot, where the archers would hide themselves. Men would then be sent to beat through the wood with dogs, driving the deer towards the ambush with the help of many blasts from the horn. In the medieval deer park the practice of driving the quarry towards the waiting huntsmen was revived. Early in the day servants would enter the covert with hounds specially trained to pick up the scent of game. Having ascertained the locations of suitable fallow bucks, these 'scouts' would report back to the master of game, whose job it was to select the most promising animal. Once the hunters were in place, hounds and beaters – the *battue* – would be sent to flush out the beast, which would then be chased round the park by hounds and horsemen who drove it towards the stand where the monarch, nobles or their guests stood waiting to shoot it with crossbows. There was much praise for the master-of-game who could provide a string of spirited bucks for the delectation of his lord and party.

Hunting techniques became ever more refined and complex. Often the quarry was driven towards the waiting huntsmen via a system of hedges or fences, as shown in this illustration from the French publication *La chasse à la haie*.

Dogs were a prominent feature of deer-hunting, as shown in this *c*.1660 painting *Death of a Buck*. The gory scene is set at Lyme Park: the Cage, a tower from which the hunt could be followed, can be seen clearly on the horizon.

A number of different dogs were used for hunting, including greyhounds, bloodhounds or 'limers', and 'teasers', small hounds which teased out bucks hidden in dense woods or thickets. This was the form of hunting favoured by Queen Elizabeth I. Like her father, the queen hugely enjoyed hunting and one of her greatest pleasures was to loose arrows at the fleeing deer while her court musicians kept up a constant accompaniment of songs and music. London's Green Park was among her favourite hunting parks, although in her later years she would often hunt in the private deer park of one of her noble lords where, positioned in a well-chosen spot and surrounded by the court musicians, she would wait for the deer to be driven past her. In the summer of 1591 Elizabeth paid a visit to Cowdray in Sussex, the country seat of Viscount Montague. Early one morning she 'took horse, with all her traine, and rode into the parke; where was a delicate bowre prepared, under which were her Highness's musicians placed, and a cross-bowe by a nymph, with a sweet song delivered to her hands, to shoote at the deere, about some thirtie in number, put into a paddock, of which number she killed three or four, and the Countesse of Kildare one'.

At times the queen's fondness for slaughter failed to meet with the absolute approval of her host. While hunting was a regular occurrence in most deer parks, it was not their prime purpose and, as we have seen, most were established to secure a regular supply of venison and timber. When, in 1573, Elizabeth visited the park at Berkeley Castle in Gloucestershire and killed 27 stags in a single day's hunting, the owner, Lord Berkeley, was clearly displeased about the loss of his valuable stock. His disapproval was later to earn the sinister rebuke that he had better keep 'a wary watch over his words and actions' if he wished to retain his castle and his head.

Nor was it just deer that were hunted in the parks. The wild boar, a beast potentially far more dangerous than any species of deer, was also an esteemed quarry, particularly for royalty. An indigenous species, it was once widespread across much of Britain, but was severely affected by the clearance of the wildwood. The royal forests and parks were among its last strongholds, and in the thirteenth century both John and Henry III are known to have despatched their hunters to Pickering Forest in Yorkshire to 'harvest' dozens of wild swine for feasts and banquets. Wild boar would feed at night in open glades and on farmland, preferring to lie up in thick cover during the day. They would burst forth when disturbed or challenged, and made for testing – and risky – sport. The species was eventually hunted to extinction during the early seventeenth century, anecdotal history claiming that the last native wild boar was killed by James I in Windsor Park in 1617.

Under the Tudors the coursing of deer became popular. Henry VIII is said to have been fond of coursing, and a deer course is known to have existed at Hampton Court in 1537. At another royal property – Windsor Little Park – a banana-shaped deer course is shown on a map of 1607. In coursing a pair of dogs, usually greyhounds, were pitted against each other in pursuit of a deer. There were two kinds of contest: a breathing course, in which the deer (only one was used at a time) would be chased and allowed to escape back into the park at the end, and a fleshing course, in which the animal would be killed. In both cases the unfortunate beast would be initially harried and driven down the course by terriers or 'teasers', but as soon as it passed the starting point the two greyhounds, on the backs of which considerable sums of money could be riding, were slipped from their collars by their handler or 'slipper'. They would then pursue the deer to

the end of the course, the latter marked by a wide ditch over which the deer could leap to safety (or not, in the case of 'fleshing'). The greyhound closest to the deer at this point was adjudged the winner.

During the seventeenth century deer coursing clearly became something of a fad, and one contemporary writer was in no doubt about its popularity among the upper classes:

> Coursing with greyhounds is a recreation in great esteem with many gentlemen. It affords greater pleasure than hunting in some respects. As, first, because it is sooner ended. Secondly, it does not require so much toil. Thirdly, the game is for the most part always in sight. Fourthly, in regard to the delicate qualities and shape of the greyhound.

In terms of design deer courses appear to have been fairly standard; a mile long and quarter-of-a-mile or so wide, although they were sometimes wider at the finishing point than at the start, so as to afford a better view for spectators. They were often temporary affairs, created for a specific event or entertainment, and there were probably never more than a handful of permanent courses. One of the few surviving examples is at the National Trust's Lodge Park in Gloucestershire. It was established in 1634 by John 'Crump' Dutton, who had inherited the nearby Sherborne estate and as a young man set about acquiring the necessary parcels of land to create his 'New Park'. Here he built a deer course, along with a grand and ornate lodge from which he and his friends could watch the grisly contests.

Parks were also the venue – although not exclusively so – of the sport of falconry, which was popular with royalty and nobles alike until the development of effective firearms in the seventeenth century. So highly prized were certain birds of prey that during the 1300s those found taking a wild falcon or interfering with its nest were liable to the death penalty. Various species of hawk and falcon were used, depending on the status of the sportsman (only the king had the right to fly a gyr falcon, for example) and on the desired quarry: peregrine falcons were flown at prey such as pigeons and

The grandstand at Lodge Park was built at the height of the seventeenth-century vogue for deer-coursing. Following various later, and rather unsympathetic, alterations, it has been carefully restored by the National Trust.

Elizabeth I was an enthusiastic huntswoman. This scene of the queen hawking with her courtiers is taken from Turberville's 1576 *Booke of Faulconrie*, the leading contemporary tome on the subject.

Every year, around midsummer, the famous red deer stags at Lyme Park were traditionally driven through a pond and counted. This lithograph dates from *c*.1750.

ducks (and even at much larger birds, such as herons), stooping down from a great height and often killing them outright in mid-air. Goshawks and the smaller sparrowhawk were used against ground-based prey such as rabbits and pheasants, and merlins – usually flown by women – were set at small passerines like finches and larks.

The decline of deer parks

Deer as a function of parks gradually went into decline. Hunting became less of a royal preoccupation during the late sixteenth and seventeeth centuries and, as deer parks were costly to maintain, many of them fell into disuse at this time. Some were converted to woodland, the name 'Park Wood' testifying to their earlier function, while others were taken into agriculture, especially where the trees had been damaged or destroyed by deer. For example, the former park at Blagdon on Cranborne Chase, Dorset, was ploughed up and planted with woad, a lucrative crop used for dyeing in the cloth industry. And in Cornwall Richard Carew commented in 1602 that the owners of some parks were 'making their deere leape over the pale to give bullocks place'.

The real value of many of the royal forests and deer parks now lay in their timber reserves. This was ruthlessly exploited by the crown on certain royal properties, which were stripped of their mature trees. Historian J. H. Bettey has highlighted the impact on many of the royal deer parks and forests of another issue: that of encroachment. In Wiltshire, for example, Sir Henry Baynton enclosed his own park out of royal forest land and was said to have killed the royal deer and felled the trees. Even worse, he and the royal keepers were alleged to have 'mayntayned their whole houses and families on venison, and made it theire ordinary Meate, and gave their servants no other foode'. In some localities the demise of royal parks and forests was to the disadvantage of the local communities, many of whom had enjoyed rights of pasture or similar access and now found themselves excluded by the new owners or changes in use. In the seventeenth century deer parks also took something of a beating during the English Civil War, when a combination of neglect, wilful destruction and over-exploitation of their resources further hastened their demise.

Some medieval parks did survive, often in brutalised form, as landscape parks or elements within landscapes which were becoming increasingly 'designed' and 'improved'. A handful of genuine medieval deer parks even survived unscathed into the twentieth century, one of the best examples being at Lyme in Cheshire. The park here was formerly part of the royal forest of Macclesfield and was probably enclosed around the turn of the fifteenth century. Although its encircling timber fence, or 'ryng pale', was replaced by a stone wall in 1598, the park remains essentially intact today, despite some landscaping activity during the sixteenth and early seventeenth centuries. During this period a series of park buildings was also constructed, most significant of which is the Cage, a hunting tower which replaced an earlier building on the same site. Lyme was also notable for the annual summer custom of counting the red deer stags by driving them across a pond, 'their horns moving like a wood along the water' according to one witness in 1750. The separate herds of red and fallow deer have long been a prominent and admired feature of the park and continue to thrive today under the National Trust.

However, for many deer parks the last century marked their eventual demise. Two world wars took their toll of the deer herds, many of which were slaughtered in the interests of feeding the population. Furthermore, post-Second World War taxation policies sealed the fate of many smaller estates and, along with them, their deer parks. By the late 1960s the number of parks still containing deer had dropped to an all-time low of 112.

Chapter Three

❖

From wildwood to arcadian dream

FROM WILDWOOD TO ARCADIAN DREAM

In 1828 the painter J. M. W. Turner completed a work that seemed to give a glimpse of paradise. It depicts a broad expanse of parkland, washed in a golden light that spills from the setting sun as it blazes a path across the evening sky. In the foreground a stag drinks from the shimmering lake, on which a group of swans are displaying. Clumps of trees cast long shadows across the water, while far off a church tower rises sentinel-like between a distant wood and the fiery sunset. All is complete: the day is ending and the world is drifting contentedly into night.

Turner's picture of Arcadia was set at Petworth Park in Sussex, now in the care of the National Trust. During his time it was the seat of the third Earl of Egremont, a leading patron of the arts, and during the 1820s and 1830s Turner spent much time in and around the great house. The park landscape he idealised was typical of the countryside favoured by the eighteenth-century landed class, a landscape created both for its aesthetic value and for the opportunities it offered for hunting. For all its timeless quality, the English landscape park was in fact a direct offshoot of the utilitarian deer park of the Middle Ages. Even as the idea of a private foodstore began to lose its appeal, parks took on an equally important social role in the life of an emerging nation. Medieval deer parks were essentially no more than fragments of nature – usually woodland or wood-pasture – plucked arbitrarily from their wild setting and set apart by means of the pale. At a stroke the common wildscape had been converted to private landscape. Long after they had lost their attraction as sources of food and timber, they became prized as a form of idealised nature, that self-conscious amalgam of pasture and spaced trees now characteristic of parkland. The English park was the ostentatious symbol of individual wealth, status and power, and a place of recreation and amusement. In its new setting wood-pasture was to signify both high art and multi-purpose utility, and was destined to become the mark of a civilised society – in both town and country.

The fashion for parks
The progression of the park from larder to fashionable accessory has its origins under King Henry VIII (reigned 1509–47). Until the sixteenth century landowners had lived in castles and fortified houses, but under the strong central government and judiciary of the Tudors they were able to give up their preoccupation with security and build solely for pleasure. In the old feudal society the manor house had been sited close to the village and the church, but by the time of Henry (and particularly later, during the reign of his daughter Elizabeth) those who had grown wealthy as merchants or through serving at court were often building their new and grand country houses away from the village, at the very centre of the estates that they owned. In this way they not only achieved privacy – safely distancing themselves from the lower orders in a countryside which was growing ever more crowded – but also effectively set off their new buildings to maximum advantage.

Home to some 700 deer, Petworth Park is one of 'Capability' Brown's masterpieces. It was a great source of inspiration to the artist Turner.

(Previous spread) The Lake, Petworth: Sunset, a Stag Drinking by J.M.W. Turner. Turner's atmospheric views of Petworth epitomise the halcyon world that park owners strove to create within the pale.

63

What better setting for a gracious new country house than the open, sunlit vistas of a verdant and well-stocked deer park?

Henry was a notorious and voracious collector of hunting parks, sometimes creating his own, but more often acquiring them by barter or even direct threats. He forced Archbishop Cranmer to give up several parks belonging to the see of Canterbury, among them Knole, Otford and Wimbledon, and in Middlesex he took over Hampton Court from Cardinal Wolsey, ruthlessly emparking 4000 hectares behind a pale and ditch and shutting up a number of villages in the process. A decade later he levelled an entire village to make room for parks and gardens around his new and very grand palace at Nonsuch in Surrey. He was equally active closer to London: having enclosed Whitehall Park – later to become St James's Park – in 1532, he further acquired, by compulsory exchange with Westminster Abbey, the manors of Neyte, Hyde and Ebury, later emparking them to form Hyde Park. North of London he enclosed former monastic land to create Marylebone Park, subsequently to be called Regent's Park. The dissolution of the monasteries in 1536 released thousands more hectares to those of wealth who aspired to follow Henry's example and establish a rural seat. Many of the monasteries owned deer parks, and while some were 'disparked' during the upheaval, many were passed on intact to their new owners.

By the time of his death in 1547, Henry had taken more than 200 parks into the royal portfolio, and where the monarch led the nobles strove to follow. The historian G. M. Trevelyan observed how 'every manor house of any pretensions had a deer park dotted with clumps of fine trees at various stages of growth, the whole enclosed by a high wooden pale. Sometimes two parks – one for fallow deer and one for red – diminished the arable land of the demesne, and sometimes...the common lands of the village. On hunting mornings, the chime of hounds "matched in mouth like bells" chased the deer round and round the enclosure, while the gentlemen and ladies of the manor and their guests followed easily on horseback.' The fashion for owning two parks stemmed from the different temperament of the red and fallow deer: although the fallow produced tasty venison, it was not the favoured quarry animal, being rather too trusting for good sport. For good hunting, the wilder and more challenging red deer was much more popular.

The march of the park pale across lowland England provoked widespread discontent, coming as it did when large areas of waste and common land were being enclosed for agriculture, particularly sheep farming. The sixteenth-century historian William Harrison railed against the closing up of good land for no better purpose than to provide pleasure for the few:

> The circuite of these inclosures in lyke maner containe oft
> times a walke of foure or five myles, and sometimes more or
> lesse, whereby it is to be seene what store of ground is

Charlecote has been home to the Lucy family for over 700 years. The house, shown here in a *c*.1696 painting, sits at the heart of the medieval deer park – in which Shakespeare was once alleged to have been caught poaching.

employed upon that vayne comoditie which bringeth no maner of gaine or profit to the owner, sith they comonlye give awaye their fleshe, never taking penny for the same, because venission in England is neither bought nor soulde by the right owner, but maintained only for hys pleasure, to the no smal decay of husbandry, and diminution of mankinde.

Harrison might as well have tried to stop the tide. While many older parks were being converted to agriculture or woodland, the desire to enclose fresh deer land seemed unquenchable. The possession of land denoted wealth and status, particularly so when the owner could afford to devote it to something as frivolous as a deer park. During the years following the dissolution of the monasteries an estimated one-third of the land of England changed hands, prompting an irrevocable change in land use patterns. In the subsequent enthusiasm for a gracious rural lifestyle, more country houses were built in the half century between 1570 and 1620 than in any other period in history. Many of the grandest examples were surrounded by deer parks.

Lord Burghley, the Lord High Treasurer, completed his great house Theobalds in Hertfordshire, setting it in a park eight miles in circumference. He is said to have spent almost as much on the park and gardens as on the house itself. Holdenby, the great Elizabethan house of Sir Christopher Hatton in Northamptonshire, was set in a park of 240 hectares, enclosed by a pale that encircled both the house and gardens. The park had become the required setting for the grand country house, whose purpose, according to Lord Burghley, was simply to give pleasure. By the beginning of the seventeenth century the diarist Fynes Moryson was able to state that any man with an income of £500 or more had a deer park:

> The English are so naturally inclined to pleasure, as there is no countrie…wherein the Gentlemen and Lords have so many and large Parkes onely reserved for the pleasure of hunting, or where all sorts of men alot so much ground about their houses for pleasure of gardens and orchards.

Wood-pasture, the vegetation of much of the original wild forest, had now become an adjunct to that high pinnacle of the domestic arts, the grand house. It had been transformed into a kind of social green belt, a half-tamed countryside separating the plain, working fieldscape of agriculture from the ordered prettiness of the pleasure garden. Under the influence of legendary garden designers like Lancelot 'Capability' Brown, parkland would eventually be led up to the very walls of the house. Yet for a while it was the garden that was the main preoccupation.

The grand design
Throughout the seventeenth century the gardens of Britain's country houses evolved along rigid, geometrical lines, imitating the great formal gardens of France.

Designers devised ever more complex sequences of walled compartments, laid out with terraces, gravelled walkways, parterres filled with flowers planted with military precision, glistening fountains, dark grottos and graceful statues. Sometimes these vast formal gardens, with their precisely trimmed hedges and ambitious topiary, seemed to dominate the very house itself. But since Tudor times they had remained safely enclosed behind high walls which effectively separated them from the park. The only way to see out was from a mount – an artificial hillock – or from a gazebo or a raised terrace. After the Restoration in 1660, the owners of some of England's grandest houses began seeking ways of breaking down this divide and bringing a glimpse of the park into the garden. And once more they took their inspiration from across the English Channel.

King Charles II returned from his enforced exile determined to emulate the grand and intimate design styles he had seen in France and Holland. Following his marriage to Catherine of Braganza in 1662, he began reshaping the gardens at

The fashion for symmetry and order in the landscape was to have a dramatic impact on many ancient parks. At Dyrham regimented avenues and formal plantings were laid out in all directions from the house, as evident in Johannes Kip's bird's-eye view of 1710.

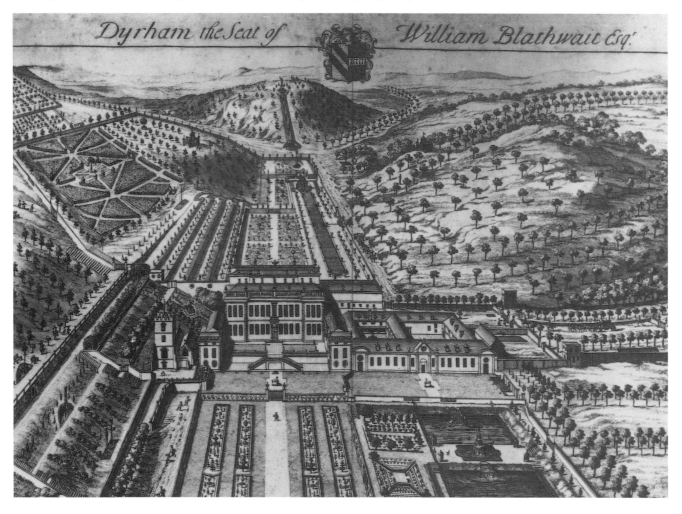

Hampton Court in royal French style, just as the famed designer André Le Nôtre was carrying out his inspired work at Versailles for Louis XIV, the 'Sun King'. Le Nôtre's influence ended the separation of garden and park. To him no stretch of parkland was so great that it could not be brought into relation with the house. His vast formal garden spilled out into the parks and forests beyond, running in a great sweep along the central axis of the chateau. This great, unified vista was reinforced by blocks of trees planted on either side, drawing the observer's eye onward into the middle distance. In response to these ideas, King Charles and the owners of many great houses began to create openings in the enclosing walls and hedges, allowing the eye to stray from the windows of the house down the broad paths of the garden and out along the broad avenues that were now marching across the open parkland.

Everywhere the builders of great houses started to think about how they might extend the principles of design into the park itself. Into the functional and largely haphazard landscape of pales and ditches, woods and launds, the English designers began to insert stately avenues of trees, canals and water features, grottos, cascades and long, meandering *allées* or swathes. They soon discovered that formal lines of trees might be used to establish a visual connection between the house and the natural features of the park, the objective being to extend the symmetry of the house and gardens out into the park in the way the French had done with their great axial gardens. As one writer put it: 'The garden was an antechamber to the park, the whole landscape became a frame for the house and a status symbol.'

It was a vision of wild, unruly nature tamed by the power of reason and art. The spirit of the Renaissance had been inscribed upon the landscape as clearly as in

The majestic avenue of beech and sycamore at Lanhydrock in Cornwall contains trees planted in the seventeenth century. Many such avenues are approaching the end of their lives, and so need careful management and timely replanting.

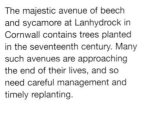

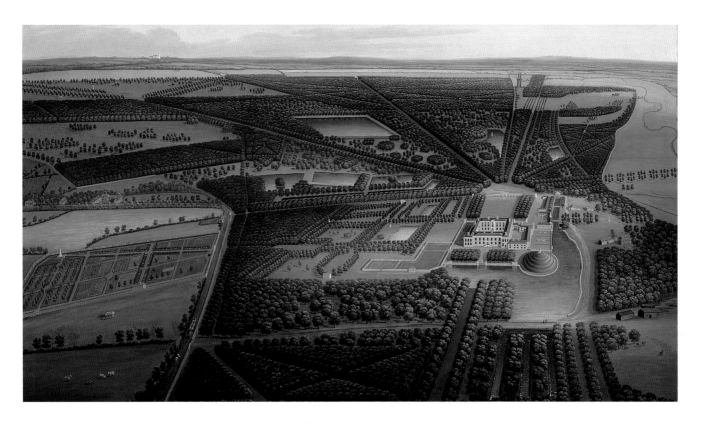

a Florentine fresco. And the great landowners of England were being inspired to do the same. At Hampton Court King Charles employed André Mollet and his brother Gabriel to plant a double avenue of lime trees on either side of a great canal, similar to that at Fontainebleau. In the reign of William and Mary two diagonal avenues were added, the group forming a *patte d'oie*, giving long vistas from the palace to the park's perimeter. By 1700 the grand avenues of Hampton Court contained over 4000 trees. Meanwhile, in Northamptonshire the first Duke of Montagu, who had been ambassador at the court of Versailles, planted an extensive network of avenues and groves stretching for several miles in all directions from his house at Boughton. When the second duke inherited the property, he is said to have considered planting an avenue of trees stretching all the way to London.

At Wimpole in Cambridgeshire the Earl of Radnor was determined that all the countryside seen from his house should be in his ownership and enlarged his park accordingly. He then planted long avenues of trees to the four points of the compass, using the house as the central axis. These radiating avenues provided shade and shelter for walks through his parkland. A dearth of trees encouraged many landowners to plant solid geometric stands broken up by axial or radial avenues. A series of radiating avenues are revealed in three 'bird's-eye' paintings of the Old Park at Dunham Massey in Cheshire, now owned by the National Trust.

The park at Dunham Massey has Norman origins, but in the early decades of the eighteenth century it was formally landscaped in a style typical of the period. The curious mound at the corner of the house may be the remains of the Norman motte.

The work of artist John Harris in the mid-eighteenth century, the pictures show six wide avenues cutting through the oak, lime and beech plantations to the south of the house. It was a landscape of grandeur and formality, the inspiration of the second Earl of Warrington. An earlier painting in the 1690s, soon after the earl had inherited, showed only two avenues planted to the south. Yet even as the earl completed the work the age of symmetry was drawing to a close.

The classical allusion

Among creators of the private landscape the slavish obedience to the rules of geometry was beginning to pall. The English aristocracy were turning against the manners and taste of the French court, seeking instead a more natural environment, one that would free them from this bondage to order and shape and perfect precision. It was a mood presaged by Milton in his *Paradise Lost*: 'So on he fares, and to the border comes of Eden, where delicious Paradise, now nearer, crowns with her enclosure green, as with a rural mound, the champaign head of a steep wilderness.'

The idealised landscapes portrayed in paintings such as this example by Domenico Fattori were to have a profound impact on parkland design. As a result, a more informal – yet still highly contrived – style replaced the rigid layouts that had been popular before.

English aristocrats embarking on the Grand Tour around the Mediterranean were much taken with the paintings of such artists as Poussin, Salvator Rosa, Pannini, Albani and Claude. They showed an idealised representation of the Italian *campagna*, peopled by Arcadian peasants and strewn with ruined temples and other classical allusions. Imbued with the spirit of romanticism, the English travellers came home determined to strip out the fussy parterres and fanciful topiary, recreating in their place the timeless Mediterranean landscape amid the rainswept hills and valleys of Britain.

Among the early pioneers of the new style was Lord Carlisle, who in 1699 had commissioned George London to design the park for his new house at Castle Howard in Yorkshire. London submitted a formal design complete with canals and a great star of intersecting avenues, which would have cut through a wooded hill. Carlisle rejected this idea and gave the job of planning the park to John Vanbrugh, who had been appointed architect for the house. He transformed the park into a vast, ornamental landscape complete with temples and obelisks, all set in open, grassy plains, here and there planted with trees. Nothing like it had been seen in England before. The park had been turned into an idealised classical landscape, with the ancient vegetation of wood-pasture now reintroduced in the guise of the Italian countryside with English oaks and beeches replacing the Mediterranean cypress trees.

In 1713 Sir Richard Temple – later Lord Cobham – engaged the brilliant surveyor and designer Charles Bridgeman to enlarge and remodel his garden at Stowe in Buckinghamshire. Though he had been trained in the formal style by Le Nôtre, Bridgeman has been credited by garden historians with the invention of the ha-ha, the sunken fence that did away with the need for an intrusive barrier between the garden and the wider countryside. In fact the construct had been used far earlier in many old formal gardens, where it had regularly tricked visitors into believing there had been no barrier between garden and landscape. However, in its early form it was used chiefly at the end of a walk to fill a relatively narrow gap in the wall surrounding a garden, whereas Bridgeman's extended ha-ha seemed to draw the whole of the surrounding countryside – woods and trees, horses and cattle – into the garden. It made possible the transformation of the true park, an area for hunting, into a landscaped park, a setting for the country house and a stage set for its occupants.

At Stowe Bridgeman used an early form of ha-ha, a stockaded ditch to unite two unconnected areas of garden, opening them up to give vistas across the park. Later he worked with Vanbrugh – now engaged by Temple to redesign the house – in extending the ha-ha to link the two areas in one complete design. In 1725 work began on a perimeter ha-ha to enclose the park completely, and make it part of the whole garden. Finally the formal, compartmentalised gardens were levelled and grassed over, taking on the character of the park itself. Bridgeman's new garden began the process of softening the harsh lines and introducing a sense of the 'natural', though it remained a self-conscious and mannered form of nature, with an octagonal lake as its chief feature, and a scattering of classical buildings designed by Vanbrugh and other architects.

Talented owner-designers were also playing their part in the garden revolution. One of the most successful was Henry Hoare, who created an artificial lake of over seven hectares in the valley of his park at Stourhead in Wiltshire. The steep hillsides surrounding the lake were planted with beech, conifers and fashionable rhododendrons, amid which he built three classical temples: the Temple of Flora on the east side, the Pantheon on the west, and the Temple of the Sun high among the trees on the south side.

While Bridgeman and others had begun the job of unravelling the intricate fabric of the formal garden, its full conversion to landscape was accomplished by William Kent. Kent was a struggling artist when he came under the influence of the rich and charismatic third Earl of Burlington who, like others of his class, was enthused with the idea of recreating the landscapes of Poussin and Albani in the lush English countryside. Kent himself had visited Italy and become steeped in

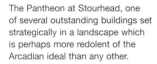

The Pantheon at Stourhead, one of several outstanding buildings set strategically in a landscape which is perhaps more redolent of the Arcadian ideal than any other.

Renaissance images, and under Burlington's patronage he began designing gardens 'without level or line', maximising the impact of natural slopes and contours and blurring the divide between garden and park. In the words of Horace Walpole, 'he leaped the fence and saw all nature as a garden'.

At Stowe Kent built on Bridgeman's tentative efforts to free the garden from its shackles of formality. He smoothed away many of his predecessor's geometrical figures, creating the Elysian Fields within which he set temples, shrines and sculptures to act as focal points in his great, flowing canvas. With Lord Burlington he transformed the formal garden of Chiswick House into a replica of the grounds of a Roman villa, with a deer paddock for ornament and a ha-ha to provide vistas across the surrounding fields and hedgerows. More than any other garden designer Kent is widely considered to be the originator of *le jardin anglais* – the landscape garden – that singularly English contribution to art and civilisation. As Walpole commented:

> The great principles on which he worked were perspective, and light and shade. Groupes of trees broke too uniform or too extensive a lawn; evergreens and woods were opposed to the glare of the champain, and where the view was less fortunate, or so much exposed as to be beheld at once, he blotted out some parts by thick shades, to divide it into variety, or to make the richest scene more enchanting by reserving it to a further advance of the spectator... He followed nature even in her faults.

The scale of Stowe is quite epic; there are over thirty individual structures and objects set in a designed landscape covering more than 400 hectares.

The formal parterre at Wimpole Hall features in a 1707 view but was later swept away by 'Capability' Brown. It has since been re-created by the National Trust and accommodates some 12,000 bedding plants.

While Kent blurred the divide between park and garden, the legendary 'Capability' Brown dispensed with both, working to create the total landscape, an idealised countryside in which the natural elements of grass and trees, light and shade, water and topography were held in glorious unity. The sheer popularity of Brown's designs with the landed class – he is thought to have been responsible for no less than 170 landscapes – marks the triumph of the park, the ultimate domestication of wood-pasture. In most cases he carried his rough-shorn turf, sparse tree clumps and flowing natural contours up to the very walls of the great house, and in doing so all but obliterated two centuries of formal garden design. In the eighteenth-century vogue for naturalism hundreds of fine, formal gardens were swept away, among them the Earl of Radnor's great garden at Wimpole. At Blenheim Brown flattened Vanbrugh and Wise's hexagonal parterre in front of the south façade of the house, replacing it with turf. But he also built a dam and created a beautiful lake, setting off Vanbrugh's magnificent bridge in its full majesty.

Brown invariably travelled on horseback to see his wealthy and aristocratic clients, earning his nickname for his usual observation that an estate had 'capabilities of improvement'. One of his early commissions was at Croome Court in Worcestershire, now managed by the National Trust. There he transformed a marshy patch of land into fine, undulating parkland by confining the water within a lake. A monument erected in 1809 pays tribute to the designer 'who by the powers of his inimitable and creative genius formed this garden scene out of a morass'.

On Brown's death in 1783, the mantle for fashionable landscape design was grasped by Humphry Repton, a former merchant with an interest in botany and architecture. In middle age he embarked on an ill-fated business venture which left him with an urgent need to make money. Born to a respected Suffolk family, he counted among his friends a number of substantial landowners, among them the Duke of Portland. With the downturn in his business fortunes he began offering his services as a landscape designer, quickly acquiring commissions. While Brown had been chiefly interested in the parkland beyond the house, Repton's main aim was to 'improve' the setting of the house itself. For each new client he would produce sketches showing the scene as it currently existed, together with an impression of how it might look if the owner were astute enough to favour him with a commission. The sketches would be gathered together into a single volume, one of Repton's 'Red Books', his famous and highly effective marketing tool.

At Attingham in Shropshire Repton designed a romantic parkland landscape to encompass the magnificent home of the second Lord Berwick, the work of architect George Steuart. To create a setting 'worthy' of the building, Repton extended the existing park beyond the nearby turnpike road, thereby inducing the traveller to believe that 'he passes through, and not at the extremity, of the park'. One of Repton's finest landscapes is at Sheringham Park in Norfolk, a work he once described as his favourite project. The park is framed by wooded hills, which act as a backdrop to the parkland.

Not that the broad sweeps of grassland and clumped tree plantings so favoured by Brown and Repton were to everyone's taste. In his *Essays on the Picturesque*, published in 1796, Sir Uvedale Price argued that their methods were 'at variance with all the principles of landscape-painting, and with the practice of all the most eminent masters'. Price considered Brown's designs monotonous, and urged that the surroundings of great houses should give the impression that they had been fashioned by 'no other hand than that of Nature'. Along with William Gilpin, he pioneered a movement that became known as the 'Picturesque' school and urged that gardens and parks should be given a wilder, more unkempt look, one that more closely matched the landscapes of the romantic painters. These ideas were put into particular practice by Gilpin's grandson, William Sawrey Gilpin, at Crom in County Fermanagh, the site of a former deer park and where he was commissioned to landscape the demesne in 1830. The result is one of the best surviving picturesque landscapes in Ireland, an artful combination of mixed naturalistic planting, romantic vistas and strategically located eye-catchers. The estate, on the shores of Lough Erne, is also a major site for wildlife conservation.

The cedar of Lebanon, a common parkland tree in Britain, is now reduced to a mere handful of veteran specimens in its native land.

The adornment of the park

Over the centuries the medieval deer park had been transformed into a landscape valued more for its aesthetic appeal than its productivity. Those deer herds that remained had become essentially ornamental, although routine culling still produced meat for the larder. The gentry also retained their passion for hunting, although by the eighteenth century the fox and the hare were more popular quarries. However, what really began to take priority was the introduction to the park of species selected for their decorative value rather than because they were particularly challenging to hunt or good to eat. As distant parts of the globe were opened up to European explorers and naturalists, so supplies of exotic plants, animals and birds became available. It became a mark of status to have one's park populated by colourful and strange trees, plants and creatures imported from foreign lands.

Some landowners even created menageries stocked with an extraordinary range of unusual beasts and birds. These were a tremendous source of interest and fascination, and for visitors were frequently the main attraction on the estate. For example, the menagerie at Osterley Park in Middlesex, a small wooded and walled 'park within a park', was described by one visitor as the 'prettiest place [she] ever saw, 'tis an absolute retreat, & filled with all sorts of curious and scarce Birds and Fowles, among the rest 2 numidian Cranes that follow like dogs, and a pair of Chinese teale that have only been seen in England before upon the India paper...' Such rapture was in marked contrast to the verdict passed by Horace Walpole on the rather flat and dull park at Osterley, which he called 'the ugliest spot of ground in the universe'.

One of the most remarkable park menageries was that created at Tring Park in Hertfordshire by Walter, 2nd Baron Rothschild, whose family had acquired the estate in 1872. A keen naturalist and collector from an early age, he assembled a huge quantity of specimen insects and birds, later housed in a zoological museum on the estate and then opened to the public in 1892. He also kept an eclectic range of wildlife in the park, including a dingo, a tame wolf, marabou storks, kiwis, cassowaries and giant tortoises. He is perhaps most famous for having once driven a team of zebras into the forecourt of Buckingham Palace.

Such interest in the exotic was nothing new. Egyptian and Canada geese – from Africa and North America respectively – had been introduced to lakes in British parks as early as the 1600s. Equally, in the first decades of the seventeenth century John Tradescant and his son, also John, had travelled extensively in the Mediterranean

The vogue for exotic creatures in the park knew few bounds. Among the more unlikely candidates was the flightless cassowary, imported from tropical Australasia and shown here in a contemporary painting by Francis Towne.

From wildwood to arcadian dream

The planting of exotic species transformed some parks and gardens. At Sheffield Park they produce a startling effect far removed from the traditional English landscape view.

region and later to Virginia, and are credited with the introduction to Britain of the lilac, acacia and occidental plane. Parkland specialities such as the holm oak, sweet chestnut and tulip tree, a native of North America, were also present in England by 1700. Yet it was during the eighteenth century that the race for the exotic really gathered pace, with many landowners specifically commissioning plant hunters and animal collectors to bring back new and colourful species for their gardens and parks. Among the 'trophies' that subsequently became standard features of parks and gardens across Britain were azaleas, magnolias, rhododendrons and camellias, as well as that most quintessential parkland tree, the cedar of Lebanon.

It is worth noting that most of these exotic trees and shrubs were usually confined to the pleasure grounds near the house, and that they were not widely planted in the park proper. Nevertheless, this interest in non-native species was to have profound implications for some parkland estates. For example, the

Brownian landscape at Sheffield Park in East Sussex was originally dominated by indigenous species of tree and shrub, but was transformed in stages by later owners planting various overlays of exotics. This evolution culminated in the establishment of the very fine collection of foreign tree species introduced to the site in the early twentieth century by the then owner, Arthur Soames. These were chosen specifically for their dramatic autumn colours, and in October and November the Japanese maples, nyssas and amelanchiers continue to provide a spectacular display.

Finding conditions in Britain to their liking, some introduced species of plant, bird and mammal soon left the confines of the parks in which they were initially 'displayed' and began to establish themselves in the wider landscape beyond. The subsequent spread of *Rhododendron ponticum*, the Canada goose and two species of deer – the muntjac and the sika – is now a cause of some concern in terms of their impact on native species and habitats, but other species have

Known as the 'Chinese teal' when it first arrived in England in the 1740s, the mandarin duck is now an established part of the British avifauna.

The scramble to adorn parkland landscapes with unusual structures led to some rather bizarre ensembles, as here with Stourhead's Bristol Cross.

become successfully naturalised with little, if any, apparent ill-effect. Among these is the mandarin duck, introduced as a parkland ornamental in the mid-eighteenth century, and now successfully established as a fully naturalised species in several parts of Britain. It still prefers parkland habitats, and the British population of some 7000 birds is of international significance, especially as the species has declined considerably in its native China and Japan.

Exotic flora and fauna are all very well, but in many senses they were just the icing on the cake. In the eighteenth century what the owners of large country estates wanted to look at more than anything was a landscape redolent of the romantic scenes they had admired in Italian paintings. To reinforce the illusion they peppered their parkland with buildings and artefacts that evoked classical themes. At Castle Howard in Yorkshire, Vanbrugh's Temple of Four Winds and Nicholas Hawksmoor's Mausoleum dominated the rolling parkland like the great stone circles of prehistory. At Stourhead in Wiltshire Henry Hoare engaged the architect Henry Flitcroft to design a series of classic replicas around the lake, many of them overlooking the garden's finest views. They included the gloriously misplaced Bristol High Cross, reconstructed from fragments gathered in the crypt of Bristol Cathedral.

Everywhere the parklands of Britain sprouted pavilions and orangeries, lodges and triumphal arches, hermitages, bathhouses, mosques, follies and grottos, obelisks and rustic seats. Ornamental lakes, many of them developed from the stew ponds of medieval parks, were crossed by elaborate and ornate bridges such as the Bridge in the Park at Bramshill in Hampshire. Many owners even attempted to heighten the antique atmosphere by creating their own Gothic ruins. A 'designer ruin' in the park at Wimpole is the creation of squire-architect Sanderson Miller, who in the 1740s built a thriving business from the supply of classical ruins to the aristocracy. Among the most dramatic is the *faux* ruined castle in the park at Hagley in Warwickshire.

One of the most enduring features of the country park is the gatehouse or lodge at the entrance. Many owners provided small buildings to accommodate the gate-keeper and his family, and these were often in the form of twin pavilions on either side of the gate, with accommodation provided in an arch above, the whole making up a form of triumphal arch. William Kent did much to establish the fashion for such buildings, with Stowe, Holkham in Norfolk and Badminton in Gloucestershire all providing fine examples. Yet these structures were more than simple adornment: they also signalled the status, power and control of those who lived within the walls or fence.

A land apart

After decades of agricultural recession, the large population increase and expanding economy of the mid-eighteenth century produced a sharp rise in farm prices and rents. While living conditions for the rural poor grew steadily worse, the fortunes of landowners – even those on a modest scale – took a turn for the better. Landlords everywhere looked for ways to cash in on the opportunities offered by demographic change and economic growth, running their estates with greater care and efficiency. With a growing divide between rich and poor, the squire and the villagers, landowners felt an even greater need to cut themselves off from the wider community. It was this desire for seclusion that provided the spur for the advance of the landscape park. What 'Capability' Brown and his contemporaries also offered was privacy.

By the late eighteenth century the English country park with its grand house and broad sweeps of grassland had become a landscape of exclusion. Its characteristic feature was a dense belt of trees stretching around the perimeter, effectively sealing it off from the outside world. This was a new park 'pale', and not one intended to keep in deer. Many parks – even those created from former deer parks – no longer contained any. Instead the perimeter belt was designed to spare the sensitivities of a social elite, protecting them from having to look out on the mean cottages of the poor. The perimeter belt might be only a few metres wide, but it could give the impression of a wooded landscape stretching away for miles.

The nineteenth century saw many owners of parks become increasingly detached – and protected – from the common hordes beyond their gates. Intruders were decidedly unwelcome, as this 1837 cartoon makes clear.

The d—l there is! well this is pleasant after running two miles, from that infernal Bull.

The new landscape park was a place where people of quality might take their leisure in the company of others like themselves. Here on the green turf with its scattered trees and carefully sited 'clumps' – small, densely planted groups of trees, circular or oval in shape – the landed classes could walk and take carriage rides along serpentine paths and drives, or indulge their passion for the popular sport of pheasant shooting. The invention and exclusive domain of a small social elite, the park of the late eighteenth century has been called 'the polite landscape'. Its owners derived their status from their possession of land and, whether peers on their great estates or members of the lesser gentry, were men set apart to govern. They were independent and leisured, enjoying incomes without having to work or engage in commerce, and although they might not actually occupy high office, they were considered to have the capacity to lead. The landscape park – with a grand mansion at its heart – was seen as their natural habitat, and although designed to give a sense of the 'natural', such parks were, of course, a wholly artificial construct. Closed off from the wider world of field and factory, village and town, the landscape park became an island of gentility.

While the park had been designed to exclude the poorer classes, it also served as a social space providing leisure and entertainment for 'the polite'. Tom Williamson has demonstrated the role of landscape parks in defining social divisions at a time when the old rural order was breaking down. For landowners the creation of parks became a unifying enterprise: almost anyone with sufficient land could afford to build a landscape park of some sort. The old divisions, emphasised by the grand and ostentatious formality of the great geometric gardens, no longer pertained. While it was possible to spend a fortune on the construction of a landscape park, every gentleman could afford a passable version. At the same time it was unavailable to the landless middle class, the fast-expanding group made up of shopkeepers, tradesmen and craftsmen together with professionals such as teachers, doctors and clergymen. Only landowners had parks. Thus the gentry and aristocracy were set apart from society as a whole, the traditional hierarchy being maintained in a world riven by economic and social change.

New lifestyles, new parks

The social changes that produced the landscape park also led to major changes in the design of country houses. Symmetry and order ceased to be so dominant and the concept of the 'rustic' grew in popularity. In the late eighteenth century, the saloon, once the greatest chamber in the house, became obsolete – replaced by the fashion to offer visitors a range of entertainments in a series of rooms arranged in a circuit. Eventually the main rooms in the country house were moved from their commanding positions on the first floor to the ground floor, which provided direct access to the gardens and park beyond.

Architectural changes were mirrored in the asymmetric, flowing design of the landscape park. Visitors could step through French windows directly into the park

and enjoy an external circuit on foot, on horseback or by chaise, curricle or phaeton. The serpentine layout of paths and driveways allowed for a full tour of the park, offering a series of carefully contrived views that slowly unfolded as the tour progressed. Guests were able to enjoy glimpses of the house from a series of constantly changing perspectives. In his *Life in the English Country House*, Mark Girouard links the interior circuit to that created outside: 'Guests or visitors, having done the circuit of the rooms, did the circuit of the grounds. Just as, at a big assembly, tea was served in one room and cards laid out in another, the exterior circuit could be varied by stopping at a temple to take tea, or at a rotunda to scan the view through a telescope, or in general by reading the inscriptions and enjoying the sentiments expressed on various monuments.'

In response to this fashion for the informal and the natural, park designers like 'Capability' Brown and his contemporaries, Nathaniel Richmond and Richard Woods, dispensed with geometric gardens and brought the landscape of grass and scattered trees up to the very walls of the house. Yet the gardens seldom disappeared entirely. Pleasure grounds with lawns and gravel paths – sometimes even flower gardens – were often retained. But they were tucked away behind the house so as not to obstruct the view of the main façade as seen from the park. The designers were attempting to recreate a classical landscape using the basic elements of grass, scattered trees and clumps, tree belts and frequently irregular serpentine lakes.

Sometimes the landscaping operation demanded substantial earth movement and construction work. A number of the great landscape parks, especially those of Brown, required the filling of canals, the lowering of hills and the raising of artificial hillocks. But generally park construction involved only small alterations to the natural topography. Owners were urged to 'consult the genius of place', to exploit existing landscape features such as mature trees and copses, working with – rather than against – the grain of the local landscape. Many landscape parks therefore retained the old ridge-and-furrow plough pattern, even when given over to broad new sweeps of grassland. When former medieval deer parks were converted to the new landscapes, ancient pollards or standard trees were routinely incorporated. So were mature hedgerow trees, although the hedge itself was usually grubbed out to provide the long, open vistas that had become the new fashion.

Wimpole in Cambridgeshire began as a medieval deer park. It was redeveloped in the mid-seventeenth century, and half a century later was converted into a formal landscape. Throughout the eighteenth century it was subject to change and reconstruction at the hands of a number of designers, including Bridgeman and Brown. Yet at the end of it all Wimpole, now cared for by the National Trust, retained its ancient ridge-and-furrow plough pattern together with a collection of mature elm trees linked genetically to those on the site in medieval times.

Devastated by the notorious Dutch elm disease, mature elms are a rare sight now in Britain. A popular wood with cabinet-makers, elm was also commonly used for floorboards and coffins due to its durability under wet conditions.

The hidden utility

The rise of the landscape park appeared to mark the triumph of aesthetic values over the purely functional. By 1800 practically every landowner of any standing had surrounded his country mansion with a sea of grassland lapping up to its very walls. Most of the deer had long gone, and the fish ponds converted to ornamental lakes. The spirit of the age required the landscape of leisure to appear natural, and the all too obvious functionality of features such as duck decoys was now considered vulgar. No gentleman would consider despoiling his cherished park with anything so practical as a rabbit warren, for example. Conceived by the Normans as a larder for meat, the park now appeared to have been given over totally to the requirement for beauty and ornament. However, things were not entirely as they seemed. The late eighteenth-century park did continue as a producer of meat, although the end product was no longer venison, pigeon or rabbit meat. It was the roast beef of old England from fine pedigree cattle.

Perhaps not surprisingly, the British aristocracy had harboured a long interest in genealogy. By the end of the eighteenth century, dogs, domestic livestock and vegetables were all being subjected to selective breeding, although the process was directed as much by fancy as by the wish to enhance some useful characteristic. For the landowner and gentleman, the business of 'improvement' was seen as a proper and worthwhile activity, particularly so in a society which viewed the natural world as a strict hierarchy with human beings firmly at the apex of everything.

Besides which, pedigree cattle looked extremely decorative in a parkland setting. A fine herd of Herefords, longhorns or Lincoln reds could add interest to the

Both productive and decorative, pedigree cattle were a prized addition to any park. This herd of longhorns, photographed with their minder in the 1880s, was kept in Calke Park.

landscape, as many contemporary painters discovered. The contented grazing of well-bred cattle seemed an appropriate form of husbandry for the English aristocrat, well versed in the pastoral traditions of the classical world. Grazing animals represented an effortless form of natural production when compared to arable farming with all its toil and exertion. Humphry Repton expressed this notion powerfully:

> Labour and hardship attend the operations of agriculture, whether cattle are tearing up the surface of the soil, or man reaping its produce…a pasture shows us the same animals enjoying rest after fatigue, while others sporting with liberty and ease excite the pleasing idea of happiness and comfort annexed to a pastoral life. Consequently, such a scene must be more in harmony with the residence of elegance and comfort, and marks a degree of affluence, so decidedly that we never see a park ploughed up, but always attribute it to poverty…

However, Repton was not entirely accurate in this observation. A number of leading landowners conducted arable farming in their parks, among them the most celebrated agriculturalist Thomas Coke of Holkham in Norfolk. Even so, in most parks the aesthetic landscape took precedence over the functional landscape of the fields. And the aesthetic landscape was universally the one in which wide sweeps of grassland were combined with trees.

In the new park landowners could benefit from the visual beauty of the landscape while enjoying a financial return from pedigree livestock. Fashion dictated that the grass in the park should be kept short. Thus owners were able to stock their land heavily, maximising their income. To manage grazing efficiently – and prevent the beautiful turf from being damaged through over-grazing – it was necessary to find some way of dividing the grassland into separate paddocks. This was not easily done. The natural look of the parkland landscape depended on broad sweeps of apparently unbroken grassland. Landowners found clever solutions by hiding fences within plantations and tree belts, using apparently aesthetic features to perform a practical function. There were other practical benefits flowing from the characteristic features of the landscape park, with its belts and clumps of trees. These were connected with the English landowners' growing obsession with a game-bird: the pheasant.

The sporting connection

Just at the time when landscape parks were being enthusiastically created by landowners large and small, the practice of game shooting was undergoing a dramatic change. In the early part of the century shooting had been a casual affair – two or three friends, accompanied by their dogs, would walk the countryside popping off shots at birds on or close to the ground. It was a form

of rough shooting, far removed from the organised and structured game shoots of today. By 1850, however, shooting had been transformed into a popular leisure activity in which large groups of people shot at birds in full flight. The change was partly the result of advances in gun design and the discovery of a means of making 'drop shot' from molten lead. Together these improvements in shooting technology meant that high-flying birds could be brought down with increased regularity.

The other major change was in the choice of target species. Earlier forms of rough shooting had concentrated on the native grey partridge, a bird which preferred to fly close to the ground and which was difficult to raise in large numbers. Now attention turned rather more to the pheasant, which had been introduced to Britain no later than the mid-eleventh century. Not only was this bird more easily reared in large numbers, but it flew high and fast, letting out a loud, cackling cry as it did so. For eighteenth-century sportsmen it offered exciting shooting. However, although the pheasant is rather more flexible in its habitat preferences than the grey partridge, it is essentially a bird of the woodland edge and so requires both areas of undergrowth and the presence of trees (in which to roost) if it is to prosper. To the landscape owner and sportsman this called for the creation of 'cover' specifically to cater for its needs.

Williamson has suggested that the need for pheasant cover was a major factor in the general upsurge in tree planting that took place in late eighteenth-century

The policing of most parks was the responsibility of the gamekeeper. Potential predators such as hawks and owls were remorselessly eradicated, and poachers were given equally short shrift.

(Above right) Pheasants were certainly present in England before the Norman Conquest, and probably became fully naturalised during the ensuing two centuries. There are various different races, and much inter-breeding between them.

England – 'Gentlemen were then obsessed with the pheasant: with breeding and killing it in ever larger numbers, and with preventing anyone else, except family and guests, from doing the same.' The gentry and their gamekeepers thought the best coverts were formed by young plantations between fifteen and twenty years old, with belts and clumps of conifers considered particularly attractive to pheasants, especially when dominated by larch. Pheasants were also considered to benefit from a well-grown under-storey of shrubs, such as those that develop beneath mature stands of beech trees. To meet this need gamekeepers planted copious quantities of bird cherry – shown in many eighteenth-century accounts – and rhododendron, planted in belts and clumps during the nineteenth century.

The disposition of the trees and shrubs was as important as their type. In relation to total area, small woods have a greater proportion of the pheasant's preferred 'edge habitat' than do large woods. So small copses and plantations usually support a greater number of pheasants than large, continuous blocks of woodland. It was such considerations that dictated the layout of the landscape park. For reasons of security it made sense to concentrate game coverts close to the house. At the same time it was logical to scatter the landscape with a number

Many Victorian and Edwardian shoots were little more than organised butchery, not just of pheasants but of any other bird or beast that happened to get in the way.

A native shrub in some parts of Britain, the widespread planting of the aromatic bird cherry as cover for game has extended its distribution considerably.

of small plantings or clumps. A more extensive area of woodland planted at the periphery would deter pheasants from straying beyond the park, and this might account, in part, for the popularity of the perimeter belt. Its principal purpose might well have been to secure the privacy of those within, but it was also useful as a holding area for straying game-birds.

Landscape parks have often been explained away as aesthetic artefacts. But 'Capability' Brown, the master park creator, argued that they should provide 'all the elegance and all the comforts that mankind wants in the country'. For the eighteenth-century landowner such comforts certainly included the opportunity for game shooting. In meeting that need the landscape park was fulfilling a far older function. In medieval times – and in the age of Elizabeth I – the country park had been the venue for hunting. The quarry then was the fallow deer. By the late eighteenth century the quarry was a high-flying bird and the crossbow had been replaced by the shotgun. But for all its aesthetic pretensions, the landscape park was still meeting the same need.

Parkland for people: landscaping the town

The recreation of Arcady in the English countryside was mirrored in the changes taking place in London's royal parks. In 1728 Queen Caroline, wife of George II, appointed Charles Bridgeman her sole gardener at Kensington Gardens, where he introduced many of the innovations seen at Stowe: wide lawns and grassy walks, formal groves and spinneys, and a bastioned ha-ha to open up the vista across Hyde Park, still largely a hunting enclosure. St James's Park, the former hunting ground of Henry VIII and Elizabeth I, had been extended and landscaped by Charles II, possibly advised by Le Nôtre. Charles had stocked it with deer and planted tree-lined avenues, finally converting a string of ponds into a long strip of water known as The Canal. The eighteenth-century yearbook *London in Miniature* observed: 'In this park are stags and fallow deer that are so tame as to take gently out of your hand, and at each end of The Mall there are stands of cows from whence the company at small expence, may be supplied with warm milk.'

While the great rural landowners were usually able to exclude the common people from their parks and retain them for their own private pleasures, the monarch could not indefinitely keep Londoners out of London parks. Although most royal parks were surrounded by walls, a growing number of citizens found ways to break in and use them. At St James's Park the gates were carefully locked at night, but more than six thousand local people were authorised key holders and thousands more held keys unofficially. As urban populations grew remorselessly, the clamour for green space became unstoppable.

While the landed classes had been creating for themselves a rural utopia, they had condemned the mass of the population to a life of abject squalor. Across the country the rise of industrialism – on the back of which many of the grandest houses and parks had been created – had brought mile upon mile of dismal back-to-back houses and crowded tenements. Inside these purpose-built slums, with their dark alleyways and grimy courtyards, daily life was exceedingly grim. Many people found escape in the street corner ale-houses and gin palaces that flourished in this morass of human misery, and in the dank and sunless streets children grew up wheezy and rickety, a universe away from the sunlit idyll of the landscape park.

Right in the heart of London, St James's Park was stocked with deer and cattle until well into the nineteenth century. This painting by W. Walker Morris shows the famous milk stall.

As working-class political movements like Chartism gained support, a fear of civil unrest, even revolution, gripped the aristocracy. Everywhere the tinder of discontent seemed to be building in the cold, cheerless streets, awaiting only a chance spark to flare up and consume the entire social order. In 1833 the Parliamentary Select Committee on Public Works concluded that urban parks would exert a 'civilising influence' on those elements of the population in greatest need of improvement. There would be contact with nature and the opportunity to meet people of other classes, thereby bringing about a reduction in social tension. One of the recommendations of the committee was the creation of a park to serve the East End of London. There followed a series of public meetings, as a result of which a petition containing thirty thousand signatures was presented to Queen Victoria in 1840. The petition stressed the high mortality rate of the district, the appalling living conditions, and the desperate need for a public park. Following the passage of the necessary legislation Victoria Park was laid out by James Pennethorne, who had worked with John Nash on Regent's Park. Victoria Park was opened in 1845, although its design was far from complete. Later additions included two lakes, a pagoda (brought from Hyde Park and re-erected on an island on the western lake), an arboretum and an ornate drinking fountain for horses.

Open spaces such as Greenwich Park provided an opportunity for hard-pressed urban populations to enjoy themselves and let off steam in what was otherwise a very crowded environment.

From wildwood to arcadian dream

The monumental entrance to Birkenhead Park testifies to the importance attached by the Victorians to their urban parks. This photograph dates from *c*.1900.

In designing new urban parks, their creators drew heavily on the rural models favoured by private landowners: the stylised form of wood-pasture that had come to epitomise the leisure landscape. Writing in the *Gardener's Magazine* of 1835, park designer and garden historian John Claudius Loudon claimed parks were as much places for horse riders and carriages as for pedestrians. He recommended an informal landscape style, with the grass grazed by deer, sheep or cattle, and proposed building a road around the circumference of the new urban park, leaving the interior for walkers:

> The road should deviate at various points to give views of the exterior or interior; the latter not intersected by too many paths. Trees should be planted in such a manner as to give the greatest views across the interior of the park while at all times concealing its road and boundary.

The Victorians saw parkland as the place where 'nature could be viewed in her loveliest garb, where the most obdurate heart may be softened'. The first great industrial city to open municipal parks was Manchester, the money being raised by public subscription. In little more than fifty years virtually every local authority in the land had come to the same view, feeling the need to provide at least one public park. The park had become a source of civic pride, an essential component of the urban fabric, an integral part of town life along with the library, the museum and the municipal baths.

The earliest urban parks represented idealised landscapes, their designers incorporating certain features of the country estate amid the squalor of unplanned industrial development. There were gardenesque features – intricately planted beds and borders which made use of new and exotic plants – and beyond these intimate areas were the broad sweeps of turf and carefully planted trees that had become the hallmarks of the English landed estate. The main design influences for these early parks came direct from the earlier landscaping ideas of Humphry Repton, John Nash and J. C. Loudon. The most important park designer of the time was Joseph Paxton, the former garden boy from Woburn who had later come to prominence as head gardener to the sixth Duke of Devonshire at Chatsworth. It was Paxton who designed Britain's first municipal park at Birkenhead, which opened in 1847. He laid out the new park in the contemporary gardenesque style, with natural undulations, winding paths and curved tree plantations, and he also incorporated broad sweeps of open grassland. With a grand mansion at its heart it would have passed for the kind of park that 'Capability' Brown had created many years before. Paxton had already designed a similar park across the River Mersey in Liverpool: Prince's Park, like Birkenhead, contained wide expanses of grass, trees and a lake, but it had been a speculative private venture linked to the sale of residential property rather than a public enterprise.

Many urban parks enjoyed their heyday during the late Victorian and Edwardian eras. This 1900 illustration of a friendly park-keeper seems a world away from the current state of some city parks.

Writing in 1852, Charles Smith described the new urban parks as 'swathes of countryside'. The larger ones should be regarded as 'enclosures of pasture with broad, well-formed walks and drives intersecting and sweeping round the whole, together with trees planted on a scale comparable with woods'. While public parks lacked the central mansion of the landscape park they were modelled on, many were gated, fenced and protected by lodges. Like the private park of the countryside, they were refuges from the outside world, in this case a hostile and threatening urban environment.

Later municipal park developments produced a reaction against the 'natural' principles of Brown and the rest. Formal beds were reintroduced, and a growing enthusiasm for horticulture produced a rash of plantings with exotic species. The simple, classical landscape of grassland and trees had begun to look dull to the citizens of a bold Victorian age. They wanted more excitement and novelty. They were also looking for bare, green spaces on which to play their sports and games. But for all the changes and innovations, the landscape of grassland and scattered trees has survived as an important element in many public parks. Even into the twenty-first century the ancient landscape that is wood-pasture remains as comfortable and familiar to an urban community as it once did to a landed aristocracy.

Yet it was the ordered and uncluttered landscapes of Brown and Repton that became part of the English psyche, the model for parkland that has become almost a cliché. The park has an enduring quality, a sense of tranquillity, resting as it does between the fervour of the built environment and the earnest productivity of the agricultural landscape. Parkland has become a kind of shorthand for calm and order, providing a refuge from the daily clamour of life. In the town, as in the country, it is a manicured form of wood-pasture that is widely seen as the landscape of leisure. It is a form of vegetation that stretches back to the primeval forest, even before human habitation. In historic times it has drawn heavily on the classical influences of Renaissance painters as well as the formal gardens of France and Holland. Yet it remains a landscape that is peculiarly English, somehow suited to grey skies and scudding rain clouds.

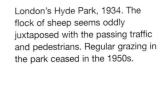

London's Hyde Park, 1934. The flock of sheep seems oddly juxtaposed with the passing traffic and pedestrians. Regular grazing in the park ceased in the 1950s.

Chapter Four

❖

The wildlife riches of parkland

THE WILDLIFE RICHES OF PARKLAND

(Previous spread) The park at Knightshayes Court in Devon contains many important specimen trees and is a rich site for wildlife.

In the 1930s entomologists searching for beetles among fallen trees in a part of Windsor Forest known as High Standing Hill made a remarkable discovery. Buried deep within an old decaying beech trunk they found a purple-tinted beetle some two centimetres long. It was a great rarity, the violet click beetle. This species is now protected by law, and in the years since its discovery has been found in the rotting interiors of a handful of mature beech trees at Windsor. The beetle's larva feeds on the 'compost' formed inside the decaying heartwood of the trees and must feed for at least two years before it pupates inside a chamber excavated from hard earth or a wood chipping.

Critically dependent on old trees, in Britain the violet click beetle remains confined to a handful of locations.

The violet click beetle is just one of hundreds of plant and animal species that rely on very old trees for their continued existence. On a crowded island where much of the land surface is constantly being disturbed by agriculture or buried beneath tarmac by developers, old parks and remnants of ancient forest represent a relatively stable environment. As a result many still retain an unusually diverse array of flora and fauna species, some of which may be very rare indeed. Sadly, aged trees are increasingly scarce in Britain. Those in most British woodlands are well under a century old, far too young for the myriad creatures that make their homes in ageing and rotting wood.

One of the few landscapes to retain old trees is that of parkland – wood-pasture – with its scattering of old pollards, together with the remnants of the old forest that was its forerunner. Only a handful of former royal forests or parts of forest still survive in anything like their original form, among them Windsor Forest and the New Forest. There are many more long-established parks with their battalions of veteran trees, Calke Park in Derbyshire being a prime example. At Calke a deer park was created in the sixteenth century, but the wood-pasture landscape there is certainly older. Old trees also survive in a number of ancient wooded commons, such as the Mens in Sussex. From a wildlife conservation point of view such sites are priceless, particularly in view of the link they provide with the primeval, natural wildwood which may once have covered most of Britain. As a result they contain dozens of species that could not exist anywhere else.

Invertebrate life of wood-pasture

Beetles have evolved a diverse set of life histories allowing them to exploit almost any potential food source on the planet. Among this colourful array of characters are many – like the violet click beetle – whose requirements make them dependent on veteran trees. No fewer than fourteen families of beetle consist mainly of species which, in their larval stages, feed on living or dead wood. The saproxylic beetles

The wildlife riches of parkland

Most species of wildlife prosper in situations where the tree canopy is partially broken, thereby allowing sunlight through. Glades such as this example in the New Forest can be real parkland 'hotspots'.

– the so-called dead-wood species – are those which live on decaying wood, or depend on some other species living on decaying wood. Almost 200 such species are characteristic of wood-pasture areas containing old trees, of which 72 are sufficiently rare to warrant British Red Data Book status.

Some of these species are widespread, and although confined to old trees at the edge of their natural range, may be less particular in their 'heartlands'. This group includes the black-headed cardinal beetle, a fairly common species in the south of England, where it is strictly confined to over-mature timber. It is much scarcer and more local in the north and west. Another group of saproxylic beetles are at their commonest in wood-pasture throughout their range, but are also sometimes found in other habitats. The remaining species are virtually confined to wood-pasture containing ancient trees and pollards, with the rarest of all limited to Britain's finest wood-pasture sites. For example, the large click beetle *Elater ferrugineus* is found only in the New Forest and in Windsor Great Park, and the beetle *Hypebaeus flavipes* is restricted to rotten oak pollards in Moccas Park, apparently ignoring over-mature maiden oaks nearby.

Decaying timber sustains a myriad of invertebrates and other wildlife, including (from left to right) sulphur tuft fungus, great grey slug, banded snail, common woodlouse, woodlouse spider, yellow staghorn fungus, centipede *Lithobius forticatus* and black-headed cardinal beetle.

More than twenty per cent of the top British sites for saproxylic beetles are owned and managed by the National Trust, with one-third of the rarest wood-pasture species having been recorded on Trust land. Among them is the hornets' nest beetle, regularly found in the hazardous place suggested by its name. Although it is almost certainly scarce, it may not be quite as rare as it appears – entomologists are understandably reluctant to venture close to its habitat to find out! Another rarity is the lime bark beetle *Ernoporus caucasicus*, found at Calke Park in Derbyshire and Clumber Park in Nottinghamshire. Croome Park in Worcestershire is another outstanding site for scarce beetles.

Old pollards on the wood-pasture 'plains' of Hatfield Forest are also of national importance for their collection of dead-wood beetles. Recent survey work has revealed the site to include 47 of the species regarded as 'indicators' of ancient forest, including endangered Red Data Book species. Among the rarest to be found so far are the click beetle *Procraerus tibialis*, which eats weevils deep inside the decaying heartwood of the ancient pollards, the beetle *Rhizophagus oblongicollis*, which feeds on decaying roots, the soldier beetle *Malthodes crassicornis*, which lives off insect larvae deep inside brown-rotten heartwood, and the big black longhorn beetle *Anoplodera scutellata*, which can reach 2.5cm in length.

The question why so many dead-wood beetles have become rare has puzzled entomologists. Although ancient wood-pasture is scarce, there is still enough in Britain to provide habitats for even the most specialised species. Peter Marren suggests that the answer may lie in woodland history. It is probable that the original wildwood teemed with beetles that are either rare today or have died out altogether as a result of climatic change or forest clearance. Of fourteen woodland species known from the fossil record to have been present in the Bronze Age, although not since, no less than eleven bred in rotten wood. In recent years the pace of change has speeded up. Over the past century and a half, twenty species of 'old forest' beetle have become extinct, including the metallic-blue stag beetle *Platycerus caraboides*. According to Marren:

> Beetles confined to a handful of old-forest sites are probably in the last stage of a long, slow decline from original abundance that has lasted thousands of years. Even relatively widespread old-forest species may be too scattered and isolated within their oases of woodland for any possible interchange between sites. Their future is linked to the wider problem of preserving the remaining scraps of medieval wood-pasture and old forest in an era when anything without commercial value is liable to destruction. When insects like the violet click beetle become extinct, the loss is not confined to science. We are taking the axe to our own pre-historic roots.

Flowers are probably as important as rotting timber to the survival of many saproxylic invertebrates in parkland and other wood-pasture areas. Flowers supply the pollen and nectar on which the adults depend for food, with hawthorn believed to be the most important nectar source in early summer. Indeed, many species of insect, including saproxylic species, appear to have evolved life cycles in which the peak of adult emergence coincides with the period when hawthorn is in blossom.

Wood-pasture is also an important habitat for a number of rare hoverflies. No fewer than nine old-forest species breed on dead-wood, with all but one being found on National Trust properties. Other rare invertebrates include the false scorpion *Dendrochernes cyrneus*, found at Ickworth Park in Suffolk, and the micro-lepidopteran *Oecophora bractella*, recorded from Hembury Woods in Devon. One of the most interesting wood-pasture specialists is *Cicadetta montana*, Britain's only species of cicada. Restricted to a few locations in the New Forest, the species was previously believed extinct in this country, only to be rediscovered in 1962. It has an extraordinary life cycle: cicada eggs are laid on the stems of trees and shrubs, the larvae subsequently dropping to the forest floor and burrowing underground, where they feed on root sap. They lead a subterranean existence for anything up to six or seven years, finally emerging as adults (a stage which lasts only six to eight weeks).

The New Forest is home to the enigmatic *Cicadetta montana*. The insects seek out warm, south-facing glades and clearings, and males will only sing when the temperature exceeds 20° C.

Ancient parkland is an important habitat for both the light crimson underwing (far left) and white-letter hairstreak, but neither species is easy to see. The underwing is both rare and immaculately camouflaged, whilst the hairstreak spends much of its time up in the canopy.

Several dozen species of moth inhabit niches commonly found in wood-pasture. The heart moth is associated with large, old trees and has been recorded at Ashstead Common in Surrey and in Windsor Forest. Richmond Park is the haunt of the double line moth, found in the grassland below veteran trees. A nationally scarce species closely associated with large mature oaks is the light crimson underwing; its larvae are camouflaged to resemble lichen, and after nocturnal feeding forays on oak leaves they rest during the day in lichen-encrusted crevices in the bark – hence the requirement for mature trees. Several moth species are dependent on the nests found in old trees, among them *Monopis fenestratella*. The species *Nemapogon variatella* is associated with the bracket fungi found on ancient trees in such wood-pasture areas as Moccas Park, Burnham Beeches in Buckinghamshire and Epping Forest in Essex.

Butterfly species are more poorly represented than moths in parkland, partly because many species are sensitive to the sward height in the pasture. In the New Forest, for example, heavy grazing in many areas has led to a near collapse in butterfly numbers. However, many butterflies – particularly fritillaries such as the high brown and pearl-bordered species – are associated with rough grazing and bracken stands. The silver-washed fritillary also frequents parkland: it lays its eggs at the base of tree trunks close to violets, to which the hatching larvae then crawl and feed. Butterfly species closely associated with trees, such as the purple hairstreak, an inhabitant of the oak canopy, and the white-letter hairstreak – which lays its eggs on elm – are relatively common in many parks, particularly where there are mature trees with widely spreading branches.

Mature trees are often the target of knife-wielding 'artists'. The incisions made can be both interesting historical documents and opportunities for fungi to enter the tissues of the tree.

Dead-wood fungi

Fungi are arguably the most mysterious of parkland inhabitants. Their appearance may be largely unpredictable, or they may appear at the same place at the same time each year. Yet it is the action of wood-rotting fungi that produce the holes and hollows on which many invertebrates depend and in which bats roost and birds nest. In this way fungi help keep the whole living system running. Parklands and old forest areas are important sites for fungi, many of which fruit on the dead or rotting wood of old trees.

Many fungi enter trees through wounds or damage – a broken bough or a gouge from a stag's antler, for example. Initials carved in bark with a penknife also make a common point of entry. However, in open forests and parkland lightning strikes are a frequent cause of wounds. Lightning usually strips away a metre or so of bark to form a triangular or strap-like scar. Into such wounds fungi can gain entry and begin their slow decomposition of the heartwood. Other fungi are endophytes, and are present within the living tissues of the tree. They need no entry point, and only become active once the tissues die; it is still not understood quite how they get into the living tissue in the first place.

Key to the recycling processes of old trees are the wood-rotting fungi, spectacular examples of which are sulphur polypore – now popular in Italian restaurants – and beefsteak fungus. Both are active in the decomposition of heartwood in old oaks, producing the red-rotten interior of over-mature trees. Fungi such as these are commonly supposed to 'attack' trees, and are decried as unwelcome intruders that devalue mature timber. Yet – as Peter Marren argues – far from damaging old trees, fungi may actually play a part in sustaining them. Writing of the trees in Windsor Park, he says:

Bracket fungi are among the most spectacular and fascinating of parkland inhabitants.
Above: Sulphur polypore
Below: *Trametes hirsuta*

> A tree may be festooned by fungi but only rarely at Windsor Park is the living tissue infected. Most fungi are decomposers, not parasites, and feed only on dead wood, which includes the heartwood at the core of the tree. If a tree with fungus-induced heart-rot can be said to be dying, then the great oaks of Windsor have been dying for most of their lives.

Indeed, far from being agents of destruction, fungi like polypores and beefsteaks actually provide a service to the tree. They help rid it of the useless burden of heartwood and other dead tissues, breaking these down and returning the nutrients contained within to the soil, from where the tree's roots can absorb them and build new tissue. In doing so they may actually help the tree recycle itself by creating a reservoir of plant nutrients within reach of the roots. In the process they convert the tree into a hollow cylinder, helping to produce a stronger, lighter supporting structure than the solid trunk, thereby reducing the burden on the roots.

Trees of over a century old are often inhabited by bracket fungi. Brackets are usually seen on middle-aged trees, and are stimulated

The wildlife riches of parkland

to grow their spectacular fruit bodies where there is a break in the living tissues enveloping the dead heartwood. On hollow trees, from which all the heartwood has rotted away, bracket fungi are rare. Old beech trees in particular often carry striking tawny and cream brackets shaped like hooves or Elizabethan frills. Most of these are perennials and belong to the genus *Ganoderma*. Like the host tree, they produce annual rings, growing bigger and bigger – a twenty-year-old *Ganoderma* may be one metre or more in diameter.

Surveys at the National Trust's parks at Killerton and Saltram in Devon have revealed their importance for wood-recycling fungi. A number of nationally scarce hollowing agents have been recorded, including *Ganoderma resinaceum* and *Perenniporia fraxinea*. The rare bracket fungus *Buglossoporus pulvinus* has been recorded at Calke Park. In Cheshire the woods at Styal are a particularly good site for fungi, including the scarce *Creolophus cirrhatus*, whilst in Somerset a segment of ancient forest, Horner Woods, is rich in those species characteristic of old woodland.

Visitors from an older world

Lichens, the odd growth forms that sometimes festoon the trunks and branches of old trees, are among the oldest plant communities to be seen in Britain. They are believed have been present during the late Pliocene period, long before successive sheets of ice spread across the land that is now Britain, and the trees of the post-Ice Age wildwood may well have been thick with them. Today air pollution has taken its toll, and many species that were common in Victorian times have become scarce. Lichens are unable to tolerate air pollution, and in a heavily industrialised country like Britain the number of sites where they flourish has greatly declined. Lichen-draped trees are now chiefly limited to where the air is cleanest, such as the western coasts of Scotland, Wales, rural northern England and the West Country, although with improved air quality there are signs of a recovery in some areas from which lichens had virtually vanished.

Lichens comprise two different and unrelated plants growing together in an intimate partnership. The bulk of the organism is made up of a fungus, with an outer layer or cortex, and an inner layer containing algal cells entangled in fungal threads. The lichen derives its nutrition from the process of photosynthesis carried out by the algal cells, the relationship between fungus and algae resulting in a more productive, longer-living plant form than either could achieve alone. The requirement to photosynthesise explains why lichens prefer well-lit places – they are particularly prolific on the older trees of wood-pastures and grow most actively when there are no leaves on the host tree to reduce incoming sunlight. Some medieval deer parks and areas of ancient forest have lichens in abundance, their strange forms decorating the trunks and branches of veteran trees. For example, Melbury Park in Dorset has more than two hundred species of epiphytic lichens, and parts of the New Forest have even more.

There are three types of lichen: fruticose, foliose and crustose. The fruticose lichens are either bushy in shape or form irregular strips and tassels attached at the base. They include many different forms, some looking like flowers or strings of sausages. One well-known genus is *Usnea*, containing about forty species. All have long stems growing from a small disc-shaped holdfast, forming tangled, hair-like threads by multiple branching. Foliose lichens form lobes and rosettes which are attached to the surface of the bark by root-like threads. They include most of the prominent grey and orange lichens found on tree trunks, and the group includes species of *Parmelia*, many of which grow grey or green rosettes. The lichen community *Parmelion laevigatae* is found chiefly on exposed upland woods in western Britain, where tree barks are leached by heavy rainfall. Lower parts of the trunk frequently support rich populations of moss. The third group, the crustose lichens, lack lobes, and look rather like the top of a cauliflower. They are more drought-resistant than other lichens, and are often found on dry bark.

The best known epiphytic lichens are the lungworts, which characterise big, old trees in relatively wet areas. The lungwort *Lobaria pulmonaria*, is the most common and forms large sheets attached at only one point to the bark. Once widespread in Britain, it is now restricted to western districts. The Lobarian community is thought to be a climax group in west European broad-leaved woodlands and tree lungwort is considered a good 'flagship' species. It is found in at least eighteen parks and areas of ancient forest owned by the National Trust. The lungwort is just one of an astonishingly diverse group of lichens: a total of seventy-seven species have been listed as characteristic of old forest areas. Their presence in an area is an indication of a long continuity of suitable conditions uninterrupted by any major disruption.

The epiphytic lichens themselves support a diverse population of specialist invertebrates, although little is yet known about them. They include the nationally scarce dotted carpet moth, which has been found at the National Trust's Cornish property, Lanhydrock. Another specialist invertebrate is the micro-moth *Aplota palpella*, which has larvae living in silken galleries and feeding on mosses growing on trees. It is known to breed on National Trust land in Scotney Park in Kent and also at Ashclyst Forest in Devon.

Parkland bats

With its veteran trees, extensive dead-wood and species-rich, unimproved grassland, the parkland habitat can provide valuable feeding and roosting sites for many species of bat. Bats need natural holes and crevices in which to roost, give birth, raise their young, form groups and hibernate, and these conditions are most likely to occur in mature trees – such as those found commonly in parkland. All bats use trees at one or other stage in their life cycles, but the importance to them of trees varies according to species and season. Some bats, such as Daubenton's and Natterer's, are most dependent on trees in summer, while others – including the rare barbastelle and Bechstein's – rely on them all year round. For these wood-dependent species veteran trees are crucial to their survival. Barbastelles in particular roost under the loose bark on tree trunks, and entomologists looking for saproxylic invertebrates in this habitat have found these bats both at Moccas Park in Herefordshire and Frithsden Beeches in Hertfordshire.

For larger bats like the high-flying noctule, serotine and two horseshoe varieties, particular features such as veteran trees are of less importance than the overall landscape type. While noctules may use suitable tree-holes for roosting, such as at the National Trust's Montacute in Somerset and at Erddig near Wrexham, large blocks of pastureland with grazing cattle are likely to prove a bigger draw. The dung invertebrates such habitats support provide rich pickings for bats and are an important determinant in whether or not bats are present at a particular site. However, while sympathetically managed parklands might support important bat populations, many parks are poor habitats.

Bat requirements are becoming better understood and action can, and is, being taken to provide the conditions under which bats might thrive rather more successfully. The key lies in ensuring habitat diversity: for example, the 'restoration' of unimproved pasture with its supporting cast of invertebrates, flowers and fungi will certainly provide greater feeding opportunities for bats. Equally, the retention

Parkland lakes are an excellent place to observe bats as they hawk for insects over the water. The noctule is one of Britain's larger species and a powerful flier. It can range widely in search of food, and migratory movements of several hundred miles have been recorded.

of standing dead and dying timber helps ensure an adequate supply of suitable roosting and breeding sites. Certainly, many National Trust parks boast an impressive list of resident bat species: Woodchester Park and its surrounding valley in Gloucestershire is a good location for bat-watching with five species being regularly recorded, while Clumber Park in Nottinghamshire is home to no fewer than seven species of bat.

The barbastelle bat is both rare and elusive. It derives its name from the French for 'small beard', a reference to the downy hair around its mouth.

Birdlife

Most of the bird species occurring regularly in parks are not found exclusively in parkland habitats. Typically they are woodland species with the ability to live in the more open conditions of a park, although conversely some may be field or grassland species which can cope with the presence of scattered trees. Most parks also contain at least some other vegetation types, such as areas of scrub, with many featuring lakes or other watery habitats, factors which further add to the diversity of birdlife. Many parks can therefore boast an impressive list of birds, although some species may be only casual visitors and others dependent on particular conditions which may or may not be fulfilled at any one time.

Many species of parkland bird are hole-nesters, attracted by the large number of large, old trees which the habitat provides. Hole-nesters can be divided into two main categories: those which excavate nesting holes themselves by breaking through the outer wood into the decay within, and those opportunistic species which occupy cavities generously provided by others. In addition, there are those species which take advantage of natural cavities. In all cases, however, there is a requirement for mature trees with decayed or rotting limbs, which not only provide nesting opportunities but are also a rich source of invertebrate food for insectivorous birds.

The diminutive lesser-spotted woodpecker is widely but thinly distributed across England and Wales.

Among the species which excavate their own holes, the three British species of woodpecker – green, great spotted and lesser spotted – are perhaps the most notable. All are regularly found in parkland (including the National Trust parks at Lanhydrock in Cornwall and Dunham Massey in Cheshire), although the lesser spotted is certainly the most unobtrusive, preferring to remain in the treetops rather more than its noisier and more colourful brotheren. Although all three species of woodpecker did well in the years following Dutch elm disease in the 1960s – due to the increase in available dead-wood and the beetles therein – numbers of the lesser spotted have since gone into freefall

Green woodpeckers are often seen on the ground, searching for ants' nests. Their loud cry or 'yaffle' was traditionally taken as an indication of imminent rain.

and it is now decidedly scarce. Both green and great spotted remain common across almost all of England and Wales, although they are rarer in Scotland and only occasional vagrants to Ireland. The anthills frequently found in parkland and wood-pasture are an additional attraction for the green woodpecker, which can often be seen hopping around on the ground harvesting ants with its long tongue (extending four times the length of its bill!).

Two other tree-climbing species find parkland much to their liking: nuthatch and treecreeper. The nuthatch is a hole-nester, and will occupy cavities already chiselled out by woodpeckers – being a smaller bird, it usually narrows the entrance by plastering it with mud. An acrobatic climber both up and down tree trunks, the nuthatch derives its name from its habit of wedging nuts into crevices in the bark and then breaking them open with blows from its powerful beak. Nuthatch numbers have been expanding in recent years and they have steadily extended their range northwards and westwards. Their noisy and bullish character contrasts dramatically with the quiet and mouse-like treecreeper, a supremely well camouflaged bird which spends almost all its time exploring tree trunks in search of insects. It systematically works its way up a trunk, often in spirals, before flying to the bottom of another tree and starting the process all over again. Often overlooked, it is a common species but is very vulnerable to severe winter weather.

Among the smaller hole-nesting species, the various members of the tit family are common parkland inhabitants, and the spotted flycatcher is also particularly associated with this habitat. A summer migrant, it is one of the last to arrive from its winter quarters in Africa and is not usually seen until the middle of May. Sadly, in recent years numbers have declined dramatically – down by at least 70 per cent in three decades – although the precise reasons behind the decline are unclear. Parklands remain something of a stronghold for the species, however.

The pied flycatcher and redstart are also characteristic parkland species. Both are summer migrants to Britain, and both show a decidedly westerly bias in their distribution – they are most plentiful in Wales, the West Country and northern

The engaging redstart is a fairly common parkland inhabitant in some areas, although rather scarce in eastern England. The male's dramatic tail plays a central role in courtship.

England. Their preferred habitat is sessile oakwood and parkland, although the redstart is rather more catholic in its choice of terrain and can be found anywhere offering suitable nestholes, including stone walls. Both species take readily to nestboxes, and on a local level their numbers can be augmented considerably by nestbox schemes. They regularly share the same territories, and even their songs bear more than a passing resemblance to each other.

Larger birds may also be found nesting in the holes of old parkland trees. These species clearly require bigger cavities and so depend on damaged or broken off limbs or on woodpecker holes that have been enlarged by the effects of rot. Jackdaws and stock doves are both common and widespread residents in such situations, as are the most frequent predatory birds of parkland: tawny owl and kestrel. Both little and barn owls also regularly frequent parks, and all these species are more prevalent where the parkland grass has been allowed to grow up so that it harbours higher numbers of small mammals. Larger birds of prey, such as buzzard and – increasingly, as a result of release programmes – red kite, will also hunt over parkland in search of carrion and prey such as rabbits and even earthworms. For nesting, however, they usually prefer denser areas of woodland than most parks can provide.

Where the grassland remains unimproved and rich in invertebrates, ancient parks make particularly good feeding areas for insect-eating birds. These can include aerial feeders like the swallow, as well as species more associated with open country habitats such as the skylark and mistle thrush. Both rook and starling are common sights foraging on park grasslands; both will breed readily in parkland trees, starlings taking full advantage of old woodpecker holes.

Finally, it is worth mentioning one species which is something of a parkland speciality, particularly in areas where hornbeam and beech are present: the hawfinch. This enigmatic and elusive bird is widely but thinly distributed across England and Wales, and is most notable for its extraordinarily powerful bill, designed to crack open the kernels of stone-fruits such as sloes and cherries. Hawfinches are also partial to hornbeam fruit and beech-mast, and one of the best chances of seeing one is to look carefully in autumn for birds foraging on the ground beneath fruiting beeches and hornbeams. The National Trust's Clumber Park is a regular site for this species.

Parkland pastures

Crucial to the whole parkland ecosystem is the grassland that surrounds the old trees. The wildlife content and value of such pastures depends on a number of factors, especially the acidity of the underlying soil. Most parks are located on neutral soils and those that have escaped the excesses of agriculture are likely to support grasses such as crested dog's-tail and herbs such as black knapweed as their key species. Parks like Calke and Dinefwr – parts of which are on acid soils – contain pastures in which sheep's fescue and common bent are the key grass species, along with plants such as sheep's sorrel and heath bedstraw. Some old acid grasslands may contain heath grass together with tormentil and devil's bit scabious. Park grasslands on lime-rich or calcareous soils are likely to feature such species as lady's bedstraw, glaucous sedge, hoary plantain and salad burnet. The calcareous grasslands at Hardwick Hall Park in Derbyshire, for example, contain the characteristic tor grass together with a range of other lime-loving species including quaking grass, harebell, glaucous sedge and meadow saxifrage.

However, it is not just the underlying soil type that determines the 'wildlife map' of park grassland. At those parkland sites deemed most valuable for wildlife, the grassland remains unimproved in the sense that it has escaped the ploughing, reseeding and regular assault with artificial fertilisers that has stripped so many species from Britain's wider countryside. Such grassland contains a great diversity of plantlife, and the more 'species-rich' a grassland is – a factor usually gauged by the number of vascular plants present – the more valuable it is deemed to be in conservation terms. Generally speaking, older pastures are more species-rich, and usually the most attractive grasslands for wildlife, with a varied structure encompassing short lawns with areas of tussocks and taller vegetation.

The largest British finch, hawfinches spend much of their time up in the canopy, but in autumn will descend and join other members of the family – such as chaffinch and brambling – to feed on fallen tree fruits.

The wildlife riches of parkland

Standing dead-wood, such as this fine relict oak in Windsor Park, is a valuable wildlife habitat and should be left in place wherever possible.

Unimproved pastures supporting semi-natural grassland also appear to have a clear link with tree health. The reasons for this connection are not fully understood, but the link is probably to do with mycorrhizal fungi, the soil-living fungi that form intimate, symbiotic associations with plant and tree roots, aiding their uptake of minerals from the soil. There is increasing evidence, however, that both ploughing and pasture improvement involving excessive use of fertilisers (both organic and inorganic) disrupts the mycorrhizal links with parkland trees, rendering them more vulnerable to the stresses of drought and disease.

One other aspect of grasslands which plays an essential role in the wider parkland ecosystem is the dead-wood that litters its surface – or at least would do so, if it were left in place more often. Nationally, dead-wood is something of a rarity these days; it is certainly in short supply in most contemporary broadleaved woodlands and equally scarce in ancient coppice woodland. The retention of dead-wood is one of the simplest and cheapest measures for helping conserve the parkland habitat – just leaving a fallen tree trunk or limb lying *in situ* provides an invaluable habitat for the myriad creatures that are part of the wood-pasture system. At some National Trust properties, such as Hatfield Forest, Dunham Massey and Studley Royal in Yorkshire, dead-wood is routinely left to play its full part in the life of the parkland. Yet this is not a straightforward issue, as dead and dying timber still attached to a standing tree can constitute a health and safety hazard. This is a particular concern for organisations like the National Trust which welcomes many thousands of visitors to its parks every year.

However, the problem should not be over-stated. It can be easily overcome by appropriate management practices – for example, trees can be made safe by selective cutting, and dead-wood does not usually cause any safety concerns when simply 'lying about'. If it does, then it can be relocated to other areas within the park where it poses less of a risk but can still fulfill its ecological function. The removal of dead-wood on the grounds that it is unsightly is rather more controversial, however. It has been argued that dead-wood 'clutter' can spoil the view in the designed sweep of a Brownian landscape park, for example, and therefore has no place there – especially as the 'traditional' practice might well have been to tidy it away. This is a misconception, of course: such landscapes were designed to be viewed from afar, so lying dead-wood would be barely visible (if at all) from a distance. Even so, all these views need to be listened to and somehow reconciled within the overall management plan for a park.

Despite their obvious wildlife value, the indications are that the current condition of many of Britain's parks actually leaves much to be desired in terms of wildlife diversity and conservation. The future survival of many species of specialist invertebrates, in particular, depends on the continuity of wood-pasture and of ancient and over-mature trees, a combination best achieved in the parkland context. Unfortunately, many surviving wood-pastures are now in trouble, along with their veteran trees and the rich mix of species they support.

Chapter Five

❖

A future for parkland

A FUTURE FOR PARKLAND

A FUTURE FOR PARKLAND

The restoration of the Palm House in Sefton Park has both encouraged more diverse use of the park and helped boost the regeneration of the local area.

So where does parkland go from here? As a landscape it has proved remarkably durable through the centuries, being reinvented constantly to suit changes in contemporary uses and tastes. Yet as the twenty-first century unfolds, the picture is rather mixed. Some manifestations of parkland are clearly doing well: for example, the form which evolved during the latter decades of the twentieth century into the 'country park' – often managed by local government bodies and frequently perched on the urban fringe – is now a firmly established part of our recreational environment. Many country parks are playing a useful role in wildlife and habitat conservation and, indeed, some have initiated innovative and highly successful habitat restoration programmes. They are a valuable educational resource and the venue for many millions of 'leisure hours' every year.

Urban parks, too, are facing a brighter future, albeit after several bleak decades. Local government cutbacks in the 1970s and 1980s pushed many of Britain's municipal parks into a twilight zone of neglect, vandalism and violence. The introduction in 1988 of compulsory competitive tendering saw the disbandment of many park gardening teams and the virtual disappearance of the post of 'park-keeper'. The concomitant loss of horticultural skills and related training opportunities made a bad situation even worse, so that by 1990 the urban park was looking doomed. However, a few championing voices began to sound the alarm bells and draw attention to what was at risk: not just recreational space, but also a rich landscape heritage and architectural features (glasshouses, bandstands etc) of undeniable quality and interest. Added to these factors were statistics demonstrating the value still attached by people to their parks: in 1995 40 per cent of the population considered themselves regular park users, amounting to some eight million park visits each day.

The hope of salvation for public parks came in 1996 with the creation of the Heritage Lottery Fund's Urban Parks Programme, through which the restoration of over 190 of Britain's city and town parks was set in train to the tune of some £250 million. Tangible results are now becoming clear, no more so than in Liverpool's Sefton Park, where the superb 1896 Palm House has been restored and reopened to the public. However, vast amounts of money are required to make up for the decades of underspend and neglect; for example, in January 2002 a £6.1 million grant was made by the HLF towards the restoration of Roundhay Park, a former medieval deer park in Leeds with an early nineteenth-century landscape and interesting features such as a castle folly and ornate shelters. And this is only one of very many deserving cases. The potential cost of bringing back Britain's public parks from the brink is estimated by some authorities to be in the region of £3.5 billion, which may be more than is considered ultimately justified. Some urban parks remain bleak and unforgiving places, mere shadows of their former selves, but in the short to medium term there are certainly grounds for optimism.

(Previous spread) Castle Coole in Northern Ireland sits within a wooded park that was landscaped in the late eighteenth century. Careful management is required to maintain the park's appearance, historical integrity and wildlife value.

Much of the parkland at Croome Court was put under the plough during the twentieth century. Work is now underway to restore it to something like its original appearance.

The HLF has also assisted with the restoration of landscape parks, many of which underwent comprehensive and adverse change during the twentieth century in particular. As the tax burden grew, so many estate owners were forced to use their land more cost-effectively than had been the case previously. Labour costs also soared, and the ever-dwindling number of estate staff meant that it was increasingly difficult (if not impossible) to maintain parks to the standard to which they had been conceived. Consequently on many estates the condition of historical park features – such as walks, vistas, shrub borders and decorative buildings – suffered badly. The design of some parks became obscured under an overlay of agriculture and forestry or, in extreme cases, disappeared totally.

An example of the ignominious fate that befell some parks is Croome Park in Worcestershire. Croome was 'Capability' Brown's first complete landscape, and also features various exquisite park buildings and statuary by Robert Adam and James Wyatt. However, years of neglect saw the park and its buildings fall into a lamentable condition, brutalised by the presence of intrusive forestry, a Second World War airfield, a radar tracking station, a sewage farm, and the ploughing up of

much of the parkland for arable farming. Furthermore, the mansion was sold in 1948 and thus detached from the landscape design surrounding it, and the M5 motorway was later carved through the western edge of the design. Salvation came in 1996, when the National Trust acquired – with substantial HLF funding – 270 hectares of the park and began a ten-year restoration programme aimed at faithfully re-creating the landscape of 1747–1809. The parkland regime of extensive grazing is being re-established, park buildings are being restored, shrubberies cleared and replanted, water features dredged and repaired and the sequence of views and circulation routes opened up again for the first time in decades.

The restoration at Croome has, however, raised important issues regarding wildlife conservation. The Brownian lake and artificial river have, over the years, become heavily sedimented and choked with vegetation. This part of the park is now a major wildlife habitat, yet one which will be destroyed when the lake is dredged and restored to its original eighteenth-century appearance. The Trust has taken the decision to resolve this conflict of interests by creating new lagoons, reedbeds and marshland habitats along the edge of the park, and will only complete the dredging of the lake and river once the wildlife interest has successfully transferred to these new locations.

Meanwhile, what has been the fate of the oldest form of parkland, wood-pasture? The biggest threat to wood-pasture and its associated old trees is insensitive management, with the key problems being intensive agriculture and obsessive tidiness. All the evidence suggests that this is a nationwide issue. For example, the National Trust owns some of the best park and wood-pasture sites across England, Wales and Northern Ireland, yet a survey in 2000 revealed that a worrying number of these were in poor condition. The greatest areas of concern were heavy-handed agricultural practices and inappropriate stocking levels, issues that are certainly not exclusive to the Trust.

For example, the ploughing-up of old grassland in parks and its replacement with robust, fast-growing species such as perennial ryegrass was a widespread feature of the latter decades of the twentieth century. This has dramatically reduced the wildlife value of many parks, and the application at many sites of excessive nitrogen fertiliser has further encouraged these aggressive varieties to choke out the 'native' pasture flora, substantially reducing diversity. The use of pesticides to control nettles and thistles was equally harmful, and in parks where agricultural production was particularly significant, wide-spreading tree crowns and fallen dead-wood were often cut back and removed respectively so as not to shade crops and impede access by farm machinery.

As if that were not enough, the mismanagement of 'traditional' practices such as stock-grazing also appears to have had a serious impact on the wildlife in some parks. This has mainly arisen in cases where the grasslands have been excessively and consistently over-stocked. High densities of livestock can cause problems through trampling and compaction of the soil around trees, eutrophication of soil and bark, bark stripping and rubbing by animals, as well as heavy overgrazing, which can be almost as disastrous for grassland as the application of excessive fertiliser. For example, research in the fenced enclosures of the New Forest - within which overgrazing is prevented – revealed these areas to contain a variety of small mammals, while the heavily stocked grassland outside the enclosures was found to support only wood mice in any number. Yet undergrazing can also be problematic, particularly in the long term, as – if unmanaged – it can result in the excessive spread of bracken and scrub, which can smother some species of grassland flora.

An additional issue in some parks is the insufficient regeneration of trees in the past, so there are now no trees old enough to replace the veterans as they are lost – the so-called 'age class crisis'. Old trees are at particular risk in plantations, where they may have been retained because of their venerable age but have since been allowed to become overcrowded by younger trees, so they are gradually shaded out. The development of such competing growth is also a result

Veteran trees can suffer from being immersed in later planting, as with this ancient oak pollard – now surrounded by young beech – in Wiltshire's Savernake Forest.

of the long-term undergrazing of pasture, whereas overgrazing – even in the short term – can spell decline and death for old trees. There are other pressures, too: vandalism, road expansion, atmospheric pollution, drought, disease and storms. The last can often administer the *coup de grâce* to a veteran tree. For example, between 1989 and 1990 two dry summers followed by severe winter gales destroyed one per cent of the ancient oaks and six per cent of the old beech trees in the open canopy area of Moccas Park.

Many of the specialist wildlife species that depend on old trees cannot survive on individual specimens growing in isolation: as trees are lost, there must be other mature examples nearby so the species can move into other niches. To ensure their long-term survival there must be a mix of trees of all ages, providing

an unbroken succession. Generation must follow generation as inexorably as it did in the primeval forest if these unique plants and animals are to survive and flourish. It is not a question of preserving a veteran oak here and an ancient beech there: wood-pasture must be retained as a landscape if its wildlife treasures are to be protected. Yet it is equally worth retaining simply *because* of its landscape value: after all, it is the main surviving link with the habitat – wildwood – that once covered much of Britain. Furthermore, the old trees it supports are potentially a vital resource in themselves; the more elderly veterans have lived through major climate fluctuations and – as we now face the prospect of even more dramatic climate change – the genetic constitutions of these trees perhaps represent the best hope of securing stock for future trees able to cope with such change.

What, then, should we do to improve the current condition of wood-pasture in parks and ensure its survival in the future? All the studies show that grazing is central to the health of all components in the wood-pasture system, and that if we want to secure the future of the wood-pasture habitats in our parks, we need to look to the sensitive application of traditional forms of management – and especially to grazing. Grazing alters the composition of the ground vegetation, leading to a reduction in some plant species and an increase in others. In the long pastoral history of the New Forest, for example, there have been periods when the density of grazing animals has been high. This has enriched the vegetation mix by suppressing the potentially dominant purple moor-grass, along with heather and some trees and shrubs, and thereby allowing a variety of small herbs, sedges and grasses to invade and form diverse plant communities.

In areas where grazing has been carried out for a long time – as in many old-forest areas – there is a complicated relationship between grazing animals and the natural regeneration of young trees. Usually periods of natural regeneration occur when the grazing is lighter, with bramble thickets protecting the young seedlings until they become sizeable trees. In most areas of ancient forest the stocking density has fluctuated over the centuries, ensuring that periods of intense grazing are followed by more lax periods during which new trees can become established. However, in small wood-pasture areas such as ancient deer parks, overgrazing can prevent new trees from being established. As the young seedlings appear they are routinely browsed off by the animals, and after a time there are no new trees to replace the veteran trees that are lost. The parkland landscape therefore gradually reverts to one of open grassland.

Concern over the fate of Britain's veteran trees has grown in recent years and the rate of destruction has, thankfully, slowed. The Corporation of London (responsible for Epping Forest) and the National Trust were both involved in the development of the Ancient Tree Forum, which now works in partnership with the Woodland Trust to highlight the plight of ancient woodland. For example, in 2001 the Woodland Trust and the Ancient Tree Forum made formal objections to the

Knole Park, 1987. The great storm of October that year devastated millions of trees, young and old alike, and accounted for some notable veterans.

The old oak pollards of Staverton Park have survived surprisingly intact for several centuries and constitute one of the most important veteran oak communities in Britain.

proposals for the new National Football Centre near Burton upon Trent in Staffordshire. The scheme threatened a large number of ancient trees in Byrkley Park, one of Britain's most important remaining wood-pasture sites. Although the designs were eventually changed to remove the risk of damage, the case did flag up the inadequate protection still afforded to veteran trees. Central to the problem is the continued reluctance of local authorities – as at Byrkley Park – to apply Tree Preservation Orders (themselves in need of improvement if they are to be truly effective) or to place any value on trees other than in an amenity context. There are still too many holes in the net, and the Woodland Trust and others are pressing both for a full review of the legislation affecting tree protection and for a more holistic approach to the protection and management of trees within the planning environment.

Pollarding can play a central role in the management of parkland trees, but its application to older trees is not always appropriate and needs to be approached with care.

New pollards for old

As a commercial practice in woodland management, pollarding virtually stopped almost a century ago. Many areas of parkland and old forest now have large numbers of veteran pollards, but almost no younger ones to replace them. Old pollards are remarkably resilient, with many living to a great age; at Staverton Park in Suffolk, for example, the population of old oak pollards has suffered very few losses over the past hundred years. However, young trees – whether they are introduced by planting or by natural regeneration – may take centuries to develop the range of niches suitable for the lichens, invertebrates and fungi that inhabit old parks and this can result in a 'generation gap' in terms of wildlife habitat. The pollarding of trees can, however, help accelerate the process by which suitable niches are created – by creating the conditions under which specialised fungi and

This healthy hornbeam pollard at Hatfield Forest is typical of many younger trees managed under a regular pollarding cycle. This is designed to help ensure adequate succession in the future.

invertebrates are encouraged to colonise the wood rather earlier than might otherwise be the case. If carried out appropriately, this form of management does little or no harm to the trees; on the contrary, repeated pollarding is thought to extend their lives.

At Hatfield Forest the National Trust is working to bridge the generation gap. Eight species of tree were traditionally pollarded here: oak, ash, hornbeam, field maple, crab apple, hawthorn, elm and beech. The old pollards are now starting to decline, but until the late 1980s no new pollards had been created for more than two centuries. The result is a large generation gap which the Trust is now attempting to fill by creating new or 'maiden' pollards. Many of these are naturally regenerated trees that have been nursed by scrub (and therefore have avoided being grazed off). The scrub around the trees is cleared and two or three years later the trees are pollarded. The time between scrub clearance and pollarding is critical as it gives the tree time to adjust to its more exposed situation and to develop the epicormic growth – foliage sprouting from growing points lower down on the trunk – that will sustain it once the top has been removed.

Cutting techniques vary according to species. For those that tolerate cutting well – notably hawthorn and field maple – a single cut is made, but with other, more sensitive, species such as oak and ash the pollarding is phased gradually to allow the trees to recover at each stage. This is especially important when cutting trees of between 50 and 100 years of age – the so-called 'old maidens' – for the first time. Cutting is always carried out in January and February, when the trees are at their least vulnerable and before the bird nesting season. The care of old maidens is a very sensitive aspect of tree management and one in which a cautious and long-term approach is essential.

The creation of new pollards is only one aspect of parkland tree management. Equally important is the care of veteran trees which were once regularly pollarded. Although neglected pollards may live to a great age, large branches may render them unstable and prone to splitting. Two decades or so ago various attempts were made at Hatfield at 'restoring' such trees by attempting to reinstate something like their original pollarding cycle. The results were mixed, to say the least. Many trees tackled in this way deteriorated and subsequently died, and learning from this process has helped put Hatfield at the forefront of current understanding and practice in caring for old trees. Rather than brutally 'restoring' old pollards, the emphasis is now on careful and gradual reduction in the crown as a much more effective way of helping to ensure a tree's continued good health. At the end of the day, the main concern is to keep the tree alive as long as possible.

Deer in the park

Some ten per cent of the parks that had deer in 1300 still have them today. Most parks now contain only fallow deer, with a few holding red deer, and there are fewer still with introduced species such as sika. Of the twelve National Trust

Red deer grazing in Lyme Park, with Manchester and Stockport in the background. Lyme's proximity to this large conurbation makes it a popular venue for visitors.

parks containing deer, only four hold red deer (Calke, Lyme, Studley Royal and Tatton), while one contains sika (Studley Royal). In total the Trust manages between four and five thousand deer, of which 75 per cent are fallow. As the Normans discovered, fallow deer are more easily handled than red deer and, since they are relatively small, can be stocked at a higher density. Furthermore, the bucks are not threatening like red deer stags can be – an issue of particular relevance in parks open to the public.

Ecologically deer have no special contribution to make to the parkland habitat over and above that made by other grazing animals. Despite the large number of rare parkland invertebrates, only one uncommon species is thought to be specifically associated with deer in parks – the dung beetle *Aphodius zenkeri*. This species is most frequently recorded in English and Welsh parks containing deer. However, sheep can graze a park just as effectively as fallow deer and are cheaper to maintain. Yet deer carry great cultural significance. They are, perhaps, the most obvious surviving link with the medieval countryside and the reason why parks were created in the first place. Their presence in many parks today therefore enhances the cultural and historical integrity of a familiar and much-loved landscape.

Deer also have strong aesthetic appeal. In Britain there are at least 70 parks with deer currently open to the public, and in many cases the deer are regarded primarily by their owners as an important visitor attraction. For many visitors they provide a rare opportunity to see large 'wild' animals, even if it is only a fleeting glimpse through the parkland trees. The decorative quality of the fallow deer in particular is significant in this respect; they have the added attraction of varied markings, ranging from black, through 'common' – a brown summer coat with white spots – and 'menil', a pale version of 'common', to white. In some parks all colours are represented, but most owners select for one particular type. This can make for dramatic impact *en masse*, as at Houghton Hall in Norfolk, where selective management has achieved a wholly white herd numbering over 1000 individuals. Visitors to parks seldom create any serious disturbance to deer, although uncontrolled dogs can sometimes cause injury or death. At some parks, such as the National Trust's Dyrham Park, near Bath, dogs have been banned altogether for this reason. Visitors are also urged to avoid 'rescuing' fawns found hiding in long grass or undergrowth – the doe is almost certainly nearby and will return to her young once danger has passed.

The sika deer was introduced to British parks from the Far East in the mid-nineteenth century. It is now a naturalised species in some areas and has even started interbreeding with red deer.

Until recently the management of deer in parks was a haphazard business. Park deer attract no subsidies and are often a net drain on the resources of an estate. In a bid to reduce losses, some owners have set out to maximise venison production. Through the selective culling of males, a confined deer population can be increased rapidly, but this can cause problems later. For example, in the 1980s a number of parks suffered mass 'die-offs' – especially of fallow bucks – as a result of overstocking and underfeeding. To help address the issues behind

this problem, the National Trust established a series of guidelines for deer-keeping. For example, no park should contain more deer and livestock than can be supported in summer by natural, home-grown forage, and ideally there should be far fewer. Unless the stocking rate is very low, supplementary feed such as hay or silage must be supplied in winter, although mature and fruiting mast trees – oaks, horse chestnut, sweet chestnut and beech – will make a contribution. Finally, low carcass weights in autumn – less than 24 kilos for fallow prickets, for example – are a sign that feeding needs to be quickly stepped up and numbers reduced over the longer term. Through such measures a healthy and productive deer herd can be achieved, and the income from venison sales can make a useful contribution towards the costs of park maintenance.

Restoring the wildwood

In recent years the plight of wood-pasture and ancient parkland generally has prompted a series of 'restorations', whereby attempts are made to create the conditions under which something like the original wildwood can be reinstated. For example, at Birklands Country Park in Nottinghamshire, part of the original Sherwood Forest, foresters are attempting to restore the ancient forest by gradually removing a pine plantation from around the surviving veteran oaks, some of which are over five hundred years old. The subsequent regeneration of mixed-age, oak-birch woodland was also a key objective. Forest managers were concerned that abrupt clearance of the pines – and the sudden exposure of the old oaks to direct sunlight and a new microclimate – might threaten the important invertebrate and fungal communities inhabiting dead-wood in the old trees. So the veteran trees have been released gradually from competition by the plantation pines, and the latter partially replaced by native tree species regenerating naturally. The slow and phased removal of the surrounding pines provided a period of shelter for the ancient trees, and the glades have now joined up to form small, pine-free areas, particularly in places where the old oaks are closely spaced. Within two years the larger glades were showing signs of regeneration with mixed species, including birch, rowan, holly and oak.

The emerging wood-pasture and forest has so far been produced by mechanical means, but the objective is to introduce grazing animals in future phases of the project. Meanwhile, at the National Trust's Felbrigg Hall in Norfolk, some 25 hectares of ancient deer park has recently been restored to wood-pasture as part of a ten-year Countryside Stewardship project, with grazing by cattle a central element. The deer park at Felbrigg probably dates back to the 1400s and contains many significant veteran trees, mainly beech, oak and sweet chestnut. Some of the beech may well be descendants of survivors from the original wildwood, which with the lichens, fungi and invertebrates they support are the primary reason for the site's notification as an SSSI. However, the uncontrolled growth of secondary woodland – mostly sycamore – had begun to encroach on the veteran trees, thereby shading out many of the important lichens. Furthermore, previous land uses in the deer park over many decades, ranging

from ploughing to timber production, had seriously impaired the site's diversity and wildlife value.

Under the restoration programme, the secondary woodland has been removed, reducing pressure on the older trees and also opening up the pasture areas so that a suitable sward can be established. The pasture is managed by grazing cattle, and establishing and maintaining the precise stocking rate best suited to the site has been an experimental process – and will continue to be so. Tree-planting using locally grown seed has also been a feature of the project, so that the wood-pasture will eventually complement the more open aspect of the existing parkland nearby. The overall objective is to create a mosaic of habitats so that diversity is enhanced and restored to something akin to that which may have existed on the site up until 300 years or so ago.

The magnificent park at Felbrigg in Norfolk is now being grazed by cattle once more as part of a wood-pasture restoration project.

Parks for People

The re-creation of the wildwood is just one type of future for parkland, yet it is also potentially the most fulfilling (at least for its creators!). It takes both this special landscape – and its human admirers – back to base, completing a circle in the development of parkland that has seen it evolve into various different forms over many centuries and, now, return to its original starting-point. That parkland will continue to feature in our landscapes is certain. It may even take new directions (who could have foreseen the success of modern day 'theme parks'?), but meanwhile there are pressing conservation issues facing those more traditional forms of park that survive. Many of these concerns are centred on the vulnerability of old parkland and ancient forest sites, some of which are now too small and fragmented to survive in isolation. Both they and the wood-pasture they contain need to be appreciated more thoroughly as part of the wider

Hatfield Forest's popular Wood Fair provides a contemporary insight into the former world of productivity enjoyed by such parks and forests.

landscape. Indeed, if the future of all parks – whether ancient or modern – is to be secure they must be considered in relation to their surroundings, whether these be the fields, hedges and copses of the wider countryside or the densely populated estates of the inner city.

Nowhere is this critical issue more sharply focused than at Hainault Forest on the edge of London. Hainault was once part of the royal forest of Essex and is one of the most important wood-pasture sites in Britain. However, under-management during the twentieth century saw the park become seriously degraded, with significant scrub encroachment and a deteriorating stock of veteran pollarded trees. In 1999 the majority of the forest was leased to the Woodland Trust, which has implemented a programme of proactive management aimed at rejuvenating the wood-pasture and securing the succession of veteran hornbeams (which make up 95 per cent of the trees in the forest). However, with a huge urban conurbation on the forest's doorstep, one of the key aims is also to promote and manage sustainable and diverse public use of the site. Through a Friends of the Forest network group, the Woodland Trust hopes to engage with those sections of the community which do not currently use or value the forest and thereby both secure the site's long-term future and highlight the contribution it can make to everyday life.

Community involvement is also central to the work of the National Trust. At Hatfield Forest the emphasis is very much on encouraging people to use the forest and learn from it, with activities ranging from a Friends of the Forest group to corporate volunteering and guardianship schemes. Yet arguably the most relevant and appropriate aspect of the way in which the forest is managed by the Trust is in its role as a sustainable source of marketable goods – just as it would have been several centuries ago. The produce from the pollarding and coppicing is sold to local craftspeople such as hedge-layers and hurdle-makers, there are firewood and wood chippings for sale, and timber from the felling of coppice standards is planked and dried, with much of it in demand for furniture-making. This activity continues throughout the year, but comes into particular focus at the annual Wood Fair, at which a range of site-produced goods are on sale and many wood- and parkland crafts demonstrated.

Parks have survived because people use them and value their presence. We need to ensure that this thousand-year old link continues by working even harder to integrate parks and their precursor, wood-pasture, into contemporary life. Only then will we be certain of passing on this magnificent heritage to future generations.

Parkland

PLACES TO VISIT

The National Trust cares for almost 250,000 hectares of the most beautiful countryside in England, Wales and Northern Ireland, as well as for some 600 miles of superb coastline. Many of its properties are set within outstanding historic parks, with some containing significant areas of wood-pasture. These all offer excellent opportunities for both study and relaxation.

The properties that follow are just a selection; fuller information on many more places to visit of landscape and wildlife interest is available in the National Trust *Coast & Countryside Handbook* or from the Trust's network of regional offices, details of which can be obtained from the following address:

The National Trust Membership Department, PO Box 39, Bromley, Kent, BR1 3XL tel. 0870 458 4000, fax 020 8466 6824, enquiries@thenationaltrust.org.uk

A former pollarded tree at Limpsfield Common, one of several National Trust properties open to the public along the North Downs in Surrey. Among these is Gatton Park, first emparked in 1449 and later landscaped by 'Capability' Brown in the 1760s. At Gatton the Trust has undertaken an historical landscape survey to help assess how best to preserve the ancient park, its key features and veteran trees.

County Derbyshire

Property Calke Park

The baroque mansion of Calke Abbey occupies the site of a twelfth-century priory. The landscape of the monks was largely wooded and parts of this ancient woodland were incorporated into the deer park on its creation in the seventeenth century. The park contains large numbers of old oak, beech, ash and small-leaved lime trees, and these remnants of the primeval wildwood make Calke Park a jewel in Britain's parkland treasury. With an array of specialist insect fauna adapted to life in old trees and woods, Calke is one of the foremost wildlife sites in the country and especially noted for its beetles.

The park and the house remained largely unknown to the outside world until 1985, when they were passed to the National Trust. Both have a very special atmosphere, and are managed sensitively to ensure this quality is retained.

Access
Calke lies beside the A514 at Ticknall, nine miles south of Derby. There is access to the park on most days throughout the year. The house and garden are open to visitors between April and October (charge to non-National Trust members); there is a National Trust shop and restaurant, as well as an information room. Further details are available on 01332 863822.

When to visit
High summer is a glorious time at Calke. Insect life is at its most abundant, and includes butterflies such as purple and white-letter hairstreak.

County   Carmarthenshire

Property   Dinefwr Estate

The castle at Dinefwr, now a ruin, holds a special place in the history of Wales. It was here that some of the last independent Welsh rulers of the early medieval period held court, and Dinefwr continued to be an important centre during the subsequent Anglo-Norman colonisation of Wales. The park and designed landscape surrounding the castle are equally significant, dating back over five centuries and containing magnificent trees that are direct descendants of the original wildwood. A small herd of white park cattle has been successfully reintroduced following the dispersal of the original herd when the estate was sold in 1976.

The park is a designated SSSI. Mosses and lichens abound on the ancient parkland trees, and the forest floor boasts an excellent range of plants. Many interesting species of dead-wood invertebrate have been recorded here, and the park also contains a herd of fallow deer. The estate has superb views over the River Tywi, a rich site for aquatic flora and described by one eighteenth-century visitor as 'a galaxy of picturesque beauty'.

Access
Dinefwr is on the western side of Llandeilo, off the A40. The park, house and tea-room are open most days between April and October (charge for non-National Trust members); further details are available on 01558 825912. Note: Dinefwr Castle is owned by Wildlife Trust West Wales and administered by CADW.

When to visit
Spring is superb for early plants such as primrose and wood anemone, with autumn providing stunning foliage colour.

County	Essex
Property	Hatfield Forest

First mentioned in the Domesday Book, Hatfield is a rare historic landscape – a survival, in working order, of a medieval compartmented hunting forest. A remnant of the once extensive Forest of Essex, it has escaped much of the woodland destruction that has taken place elsewhere. Today deer and cattle graze among the coppiced and pollarded trees, a living re-enactment of how the forest was managed in medieval times.

A designated National Nature Reserve, the forest is divided into sections separated by permanent woodbanks, with areas of pasture, wooded glades, footpaths and rides. Over two hundred plant species have been recorded here, and the parkland contains more than eight hundred ancient pollards of several different species. The oldest trees are almost seven hundred years old. Birdlife is equally rich, and includes hawfinch, nightingale and all three species of woodpecker.

Access
Hatfield Forest is located three miles east of Bishop's Stortford, with access to the car park via a minor road leading south from the A120 at Takeley Street (parking charge for non-National Trust members). There is open access for pedestrians with an extensive network of footpaths. Further information is available on 01279 870678.

When to visit
April and May are ideal for enjoying the spectacular display of buttercups in the wood-pasture and for listening to the extraordinary song of the nightingale.

County	Cheshire
Property	Lyme Park

A medieval deer park with extensive areas of parkland, woodland and moorland, Lyme is striking for its qualities of age and continuity. Ancient wood-pasture and formal plantings dating from the seventeenth and eighteenth centuries show clearly how the landscape has evolved, and the steeply rising ground provides a dramatic setting for Lyme Hall.

The parkland is home to two herds of deer, red and fallow. The red deer are descendants of the herd which once populated the royal hunting forest of nearby Macclesfield. Among the range of important wildlife habitats at Lyme are open rough pasture and wood-pasture, which both support a number of specialised animal and plant communities. Birds include pied flycatcher and raven.

Access
The main entrance is on the A6 six miles south-east of Stockport and seventeen miles north-west of Buxton. The park is open daily throughout the year, with the hall and garden open seasonally between April and October (charge to non-National Trust members). There are two National Trust shops, a restaurant, tea-room and information centre, all open seasonally. The Cage, a former hunting tower on the brow of a hill, is open at certain times. A network of footpaths provides splendid vistas throughout the park. Further information is available on 01663 762023.

When to visit
The deer are at their most dramatic during the autumn rut, a time when the foliage on the parkland trees is also particularly impressive.

County	Down
Property	Castle Ward

The walled park at Castle Ward enjoys a spectacular location alongside Strangford Lough. Some of the formal landscape elements – such as the long rectangular canal known as Temple Water – date back to 1728, but much of the park's current appearance is a result of extensive informal nineteenth-century planting. This provides a superb setting for one of the most curious houses in Northern Ireland, built with two facades in very different styles.

The wide variety of landscape features makes the park an important site for wildlife. Classic woodland plants such as wood sanicle and enchanter's nightshade flourish here, and the clearings attract good numbers of butterflies. Adjacent Strangford Lough is a major site for waterfowl.

Access
Off the A25, seven miles from Downpatrick and a short distance from Strangford. There is access to the park and its many walks throughout the year, with the house and Strangford Lough Wildlife Centre open from March to October only; charge for non-National Trust members. Further information is available on 028 4488 1204.

When to visit
The wide variety of trees in the park makes for spectacular viewing all year round, but May is particularly good (with excellent displays of bluebells and rhododendrons).

FURTHER READING

The following is a list of useful books and articles for those who wish to find out more about parkland. Many can be found on the shelves of public libraries, through which the more obscure titles can often be ordered.

On the history of forests, parks and wooded commons, the best titles include:
J.H. Bettey, *Estates and the English Countryside*, Batsford (1993)
James Bond, "Forests, chases, warrens and parks in medieval Wessex", in Michael Aston and Carenza Lewis (eds.), *The medieval landscape of Wessex*, Oxbow Monograph 46 (1994)
C. Hart, *The verderers and forest laws of Dean*, David and Charles (1971)
Edward T. MacDermot, *The history of the forest of Exmoor*, David and Charles Reprints (1973)
Peter Marren, *The Wild Woods*, David and Charles (1992)
Peter J. Neville Havins, *The forests of England*, Readers Union (1976)
Oliver Rackham, *The last forest*; the story of Hatfield Forest, Dent (1989)
Oliver Rackham, *Trees and woodland in the British landscape*, Dent (1976)
Simon Schama, *Landscape and memory*, Fontana (1995)
Paul Stamper, "Woods and parks", in Grenville Asthill and Annie Grant (eds.), *The countryside of medieval England*, Blackwell (1988)
Colin Tubbs, *The New Forest*, Collins (1986)

The literature on deer parks and their history is somewhat limited. The more useful titles include:
M. Baxter Brown, *Richmond Park: The history of a royal deer park*, Robert Hale (1985)
Leonard Cantor, "Forests, chases, parks and warrens", in Leonard Cantor (ed.), *The English medieval landscape*, Croom Helm (1982)
Leonard Cantor, *The medieval parks of England, A gazetteer*, Loughborough University (1983)

Frederick Hingston (ed.), *Deer parks and deer of Great Britain*, Sporting and Leisure Press (1988)
W. G. Hoskins, *The making of the English Landscape*, Hodder and Stoughton (1955)
Oliver Rackham, *The history of the countryside*, Dent (1986)
Evelyn Philip Shirley, *Some account of English deer parks*, John Murray (1867)

Parkland as a designer landscape – the story of the landscape park
Ralph Dutton, *The English garden*, Batsford (1937)
Miles Hadfield, *The English Landscape Garden*, Shire Publications (1997)
Susan Lasdun, *The English Park: Royal, private and public*, The Vendome Press (1992)
N. T. Newton, *Design on the land*, Belknap Press/Harvard University Press (1971)
Tom Williamson, "Fish, fur and feather: Man and nature in the post-medieval landscape", in Katherine Barker and Timothy Darvill (eds.), *Making English landscapes*, Bournemouth University Occasional Paper 3 (1997)
Tom Williamson, *Polite Landscapes: Gardens and Society in eighteenth-century England*, Sutton Publishing (1995)

Wildlife in parkland. Among the best publications on the subject are:
K. N. A. Alexander, "Historic parks and pasture-woodlands: The National Trust resource and its conservation", *Biological Journal of the Linnean Society*, (1995), 56 (Suppl.): 155-175
K. J. Kirby et al., "Pasture woodland and its conservation in Britain", *Biological Journal of the Linnean Society*, (1995), 56 (Suppl.): 135-153
P. Kirby, *Habitat management for invertebrates: A practical handbook*, Royal Society for the Protection of Birds (1992)
Peter Marren, *The Wild Woods* (see above)
Peter Marren, *Woodland heritage*, David and Charles (1990)

M. C. D. Speight, "Saproxylic invertebrates and their conservation", *Nature and Environment Series*, 42, Council of Europe, Strasbourg (1989)
Colin R. Tubbs, "The Ecology of Pastoralism in the New Forest", *British Wildlife*, October 1997, pp. 7-16

The survival of parkland depends on practical conservation management. The more interesting accounts include:

Paul Barwick and Andrew Powers, "Restoring the greenwood", in *Enact: Managing land for wildlife*, Vol. 8, No. 3, Autumn 2000, pp. 4-6
David Bullock and Paul Collis, "Managing deer in parklands", in *Enact: Managing land for wildlife*, Vol. 8, No. 3, Autumn 2000, pp. 11-14
Vikki Forbes and Adrian Clarke, "Bridging the generation gap", in *Enact: Managing land for wildlife*, Vol. 8, No. 3, Autumn 2000, pp. 7-9
K. J. Kirby et al., "Pasture-woodland and its conservation in Britain", *Biological Journal of the Linnean Society* (1995), 56 (Suppl.), 135-53
Tom Wall, "Strategies for nature conservation in parklands: Some examples from Moccas Park National Nature Reserve", in David J. Bullock and Keith Alexander (eds.), *Parklands – The way forward*, English Nature Research Report No. 295, p. 44
Charles Watkins, *Woodland management and conservation*, David and Charles (1990), pp. 123-4

Special events such as drama and story-telling are helping to increase popular appreciation of historic parks and forests, as here at the Woodland Trust's Hainault Forest.

NATIONAL TRUST PUBLICATIONS

The National Trust publishes a wide range of books that promote both its work and the great variety of properties in its care. In addition to more than 350 guidebooks on individual places to visit, there are currently over 70 other titles in print, covering subjects as diverse as gardening, costume, dining, country walks and heraldry. These are all available through good bookshops worldwide and via our website **www.nationaltrust.org.uk/bookshop**, as well as in National Trust shops and by mail order on 01394 389950. The Trust also runs an academic publishing programme, under which books are published on more specialised subjects such as specific conservation projects and the Trust's renowned collections of art.

Details of all National Trust publications are listed in our books catalogue, available from The National Trust, 36 Queen Anne's Gate, London SW1H 9AS – please enclose a stamped self-addressed envelope.

Parkland is the second title in the new National Trust series *Living Landscapes*. Appreciation of landscape is nothing new, but a balanced understanding of the history and value of human interaction with the environment has only come about more recently. Through *Living Landscapes* we aim to explore this interaction, drawing on the vast range of habitats and landscapes in the Trust's care and on the bank of expertise the Trust has acquired in managing both these and the wildlife they support.

Each book will explore the social and natural history of a different type of landscape or habitat: *Hedges and Walls*, the first title in the series, reveals the complex world of field boundaries, with forthcoming titles looking at the extraordinary story of our *Rivers and Canals* and at the evocative subject of *Heathland*. Beautifully illustrated with specially commissioned artwork and a range of stunning contemporary photographs and historical material, this series will appeal to all those with an interest in social history, wildlife and the environment.

Further details are available on our website (see above).

PICTURE CREDITS

Front cover	NTPL/Joe Cornish
p4	NTPL/David Sellman
pp8-9	NTPL/Charlie Waite
pp10-11	NTPL/Paul Wakefield
p12	Archie Miles
p17	Archie Miles
p20	NTPL/John Hammond
p21	Mary Evans Picture Library
p22	Mary Evans Picture Library
p26	Mary Evans Picture Library
p29	NTPL/Paul Wakefield
p30	Archie Miles
p33	Archie Miles
pp34-5	NTPL/John Hammond
p36	Mary Evans Picture Library
p38	NT/Bob Hockey
p42	Reproduced from F. Hingston, *Deer parks and deer of Great Britain*, Sporting and Leisure Press (1988)
p44	Mary Evans Picture Library
p46	NTPL/Oliver Benn
p47	Mary Evans Picture Library
p49	NT/Thames & Solent
p50	NTPL/Tymn Lintell
p52	Mary Evans Picture Library
p53	Mary Evans Picture Library
p54	NTPL/John Hammond
p56	NTPL/Nick Meers
p57	Mary Evans Picture Library
p58	NTPL/John Hammond
pp60-1	©Tate, London 2002
p62	NTPL/Ian West
p64	NTPL/Derrick E.Witty
p67	NT
p68	NTPL/Derek Croucher
p69	NTPL/Angelo Hornak
p70	NTPL/Michael Dudley
p72	NTPL/Nick Meers
p73	NTPL/Andrew Butler
pp74-5	NTPL/Nick Meers
p77	NTPL/John Hammond
p78	NTPL/Derek Croucher
p80	NTPL/Nick Meers
p81	Mary Evans Picture Library
p83	NTPL
p85	NT/East Midlands
p87	Mary Evans Picture Library
p88	Mary Evans Picture Library
p89	NT
p90	NTPL/Derrick E.Witty
p91	Mary Evans Picture Library
pp92-3	www.merseysideviews.com
p94	Mary Evans Picture Library
p95	Mary Evans Picture Library
pp96-7	NTPL/Stephen Robson
p99	Archie Miles
p104	Archie Miles
p115	Archie Miles
pp116-7	NTPL/David Noton
p119	©Chris Brink/VIEW
pp120-1	NTPL/David Noton
p123	Archie Miles
p124	NTPL/David Dixon
p126	Archie Miles
p129	NT
p131	NTPL/Mike Williams
p133	NT/Keith Zealand
p134	NT
p137	NTPL/David Sellman
p139	NTPL/Nick Meers
p141	NTPL/Andrew Butler
p143	NT
p145	NTPL/Nick Meers
p147	NTPL/Mike Williams
p148	Alex von Koettlitz/Woodland Trust Picture Library
p150	NTPL/Stephen Robson
p160	Archie Miles

Inside watercolour and pencil artwork by Dan Cole
Scraperboard artwork by Alison Lang

INDEX

C

D

(*Overleaf*) A veteran oak pollard in Savernake Forest, Wiltshire.